IS-328 Plan Review for Local Mitigation Plans

FEMA

Instructor Guide

September 2012

Cover photo is from FEMA Photo Library and shows a house in Baldwin County, Alabama that has been elevated to mitigate flood damage.

Table of Contents

INSTRUCTOR PREPARATION

This part of the Instructor Guide provides instructors with administrative, logistical, and content support to prepare for and deliver this course. Early review of this section will help you to organize and deliver this course in an effective manner.

COURSE CONTENT

Goal

The goal of this course is to provide plan approvers with the information and tools that they will need to review local hazard mitigation plans using the FEMA 2011 *Local Mitigation Plan Review Guide*.

Objectives

Upon successful completion of this course, participants will be able to:

- Explain the purpose and intent of a plan review
- Describe how to recognize elements of plans that meet plan requirements
- Describe how to use the Plan Review Tool
- Describe how to convey the results of the review using the Regulation Checklist and the Plan Assessment parts of the Plan Review Tool

COURSE OVERVIEW

Module	Objectives	Time
Introduction	<ul><li>Introduce course participants and instructors</li><li>Describe the rationale for the course and the course goal</li></ul>	20 minutes
Section1: Background	<ul><li>Describe the concepts critical for conducting plan reviews: mitigation planning, mitigation planning process, and roles of local communities, the State, and Federal Emergency Management Agency (FEMA) in reviewing a local mitigation plan</li><li>Explain the purpose and intent of the mitigation plan review</li></ul>	20 minutes

Module	Objectives	Time
Section 2: Guiding Principles	• Describe the Guiding Principles that are important to keep in mind while doing a plan review to ensure that reviews are fair and reasonable	20 minutes
Section 3: Overview of Plan Review Resources	• Describe the content of the Plan Review Tool • Describe how to use the Plan Review Tool	0.5 hours
Section 4: Regulation Checklist	• Describe how to recognize elements of plans that meet plan requirements • Describe how to convey the results of the review using the Regulation Checklist	0.5 hours
Section 5: Plan Assessment	• Describe how to convey the results of the review using the Plan Assessment	0.5 hours
Section 6: Wrap-up and Post-Course Assessment	• Review course goals and objectives • Ask questions and clarify remaining issues • Assess understanding of the concepts presented in this course	0.5 hours

TARGET AUDIENCE

This course is designed for new and experienced State and FEMA plan reviewers. Plan reviewers may be full-time or FEMA Disaster Assistance Employees, FEMA contract plan reviewers, or State plan reviewers.

REQUIRED PREREQUISITES

Participants are not required to complete any specific courses as prerequisites to this course. However, course IS 318: Hazard Mitigation Planning is recommended.

INSTRUCTORS

For offerings at the Emergency Management Institute (EMI), the Course Manager, who is responsible for scheduling and managing the overall course delivery, will manage the course.

For field offerings, the Lead Instructor will be responsible for this effort if the EMI Course Manager is not available. Selecting a Lead Instructor from the pool of instructors is recommended. The Lead Instructor:

- Provides the class with prompt feedback on subject matter issue resolutions

- Serves as a tabletop leader during group activities

- Facilitates discussion of subject issues arising among the instructor group

- Facilitates discussion of the participants' evaluation, and resolves any items relating to the accuracy of the content of the course

- Establishes a contact at FEMA Headquarters to discuss questions that could not be not answered and other potential issues

Instructors will ensure that they:

- Are familiar with all course materials

- Have a copy of the course agenda

- Are able to discuss current policy and program changes

- Have updated the section examples to remain timely

- Are current with their instructional skills

QUALIFICATIONS

This course is designed to be taught by FEMA instructors who have extensive and current experience reviewing local hazard mitigation plans, with knowledge of plan development as well as the plan approval process.

All instructors must demonstrate effective instructional skills, be able to communicate effectively with the target audience, and be able to adhere to time schedules.

METHODOLOGY

This course is designed for delivery in the classroom. The course delivery will be most effective if each student has some experience with local hazard mitigation plan review and has an understanding of local hazard mitigation planning.

The course is broken into six sections. Each instructional unit combines informal lecture with opportunities for participant questions and observations.

Course instructors will facilitate discussions and provide immediate feedback to participant questions. Participants will be required to demonstrate their comprehension of the skills and knowledge through an individual post-course assessment.

DURATION

This format allows the course to be delivered in 4 hours of instruction, which includes lecture, breaks, and a post-course assessment.

COURSE AGENDA

Time	Day 1
8:30 – 9:30	Introduction, Sections 1 and 2
9:30 – 9:45	Break
9:45 – 10:45	Sections 3 and 4
10:45 – 11:00	Break
11:00 – 12:00	Sections 5 and 6
12:00 – 1:00	Lunch

PREPARATION CHECKLIST

Pre-Delivery Administrative Duties

- Obtain the course roster
- Download and print course materials and a copy of the FEMA 2011 *Local Mitigation Plan Review Guide*
- Select ten questions from the list of questions provided in the Instructor Guide on pages IG-118 through IG-124 to create a Post-Course Assessment
- Make the appropriate number of copies of the Student Guide and the Post-Course Assessment

Pre-Delivery Instructor Preparation

Your preparation has a direct impact on training effectiveness. Use the following steps during your preparation:

- Read the Instructor Guide and the Student Manual thoroughly
- Be prepared to answer any questions that participants may ask
- Draft your own notes in the white space around the margins in the Instructor Guide; sharing personal experiences helps illustrate course concepts

Using This Manual

This manual has been formatted to facilitate course delivery. Key features include:

- Instructor Notes that provide helpful directions
- Instructor Note icons to identify information that is not part of the Student Guide

> ♪   Instructor Note

CLASSROOM SETUP AND FACILITY REQUIREMENTS

The following space requirements are recommended:

- Room dimensions for class of 25–30 participants are a minimum of 1,250 square (e.g., 25 feet x 50 feet)

- Five to six tables, seating five to six people per table

- Instructor table to accommodate assigned instructors

- Additional space/tables for materials and supplies, audio-visual/electronic equipment (projector, etc.), and break foods (coffee, snacks)

SUPPLIES AND EQUIPMENT

Audio-Visual/Electronic Equipment

- Computer with PowerPoint software for instructor

- LCD projector and large projection screen

- Overhead projector and screen (optional or as a backup)

- Handheld microphones (two per class)

- Lapel microphones for instructors (minimum of two)

- Laser pointer

Classroom Materials

- Tables and chairs

- Easel pads, felt-tipped markers, and stands

- Administrative Materials

- Name tags and name tents for each participant and instructor

Participant Supplies

- Pads of paper (8.5- x 11-inch size) (one per participant and instructor)

- Highlighters for participants (minimum one per participant)

- Pencils and pens

- Post-It notes

Instructional Materials

Course materials include Instructor Guide, Student Manual, handouts, and visuals. See the following table for print instructions.

Requires Copying	Item	Quantity
✓	Instructor Guide	(Instructors: one each)
✓	Student Manual	(Enrolled participants + 1*)
✓	Course Evaluations	(Enrolled participants)
✓	Post-Course Assessment	(Enrolled participants)

*Extra Student Manual intended for instructor reference.

EVALUATION

Level I: At EMI offerings, the EMI Course Evaluation Form will be used to document participant feedback on the overall quality of the content, the instruction, and the facilities. The form uses a 1 to 5 rating system, with 5 being the highest. At the end of the course, the Course Manager will lead a feedback session so participants also have the opportunity to provide verbal feedback on the course content.

Level II: A Student Assessment will be performed to assess the participants' ability to demonstrate proficiency in applying the program knowledge and skills needed to complete a plan review.

SUPPORTING PUBLICATION

The FEMA 2011 *Local Mitigation Plan Review Guide* supports the course materials and should be used to increase understanding of the material presented.

INTRODUCTION

Time: 20 minutes

OBJECTIVES

At the end of this section, participants will be able to:

- Describe the rationale for the course and course goal
- Be familiar with the instructor and fellow participants

METHODOLOGY

This section includes lecture and provides an opportunity for participants to ask questions.

IS-328 Plan Review for Local Mitigation Plans

Visual 1

Administrative

- Emergency exits
- Restrooms
- Cell phones
- Course materials

Please note the location of emergency exits and restrooms.

Please be courteous and turn off or silence cell phones and other electronic communications devices. If you have an emergency and must take a call, please leave the classroom quietly.

Please do not "talk over" others or be disagreeable in your interactions with other students or the instructors.

Each participant should have a Student Guide and a printed copy of the FEMA 2011 *Local Mitigation Plan Review Guide* (Plan Review Guide) for reference during the course.

 Photo shows hurricane damage in Connecticut.

All photos used in this presentation are from FEMA's Photo Library or from the FEMA Map Service Center.

Visual 2

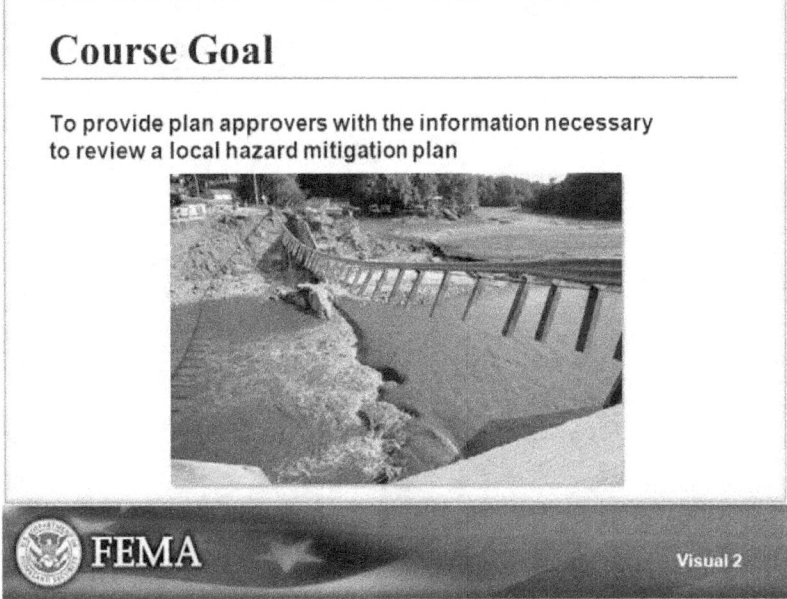

Course Goal:

- To provide plan approvers with the information necessary to review a local hazard mitigation plan

The goal of the course is to provide plan approvers with the information that they will need to review local hazard mitigation plans using the Plan Review Guide.

♪	Photo shows a failed dam in Iowa.

Visual 3

Objectives

At the end of this course, participants will be able to

A. Explain the purpose and intent of reviewing Local Mitigation Plans

B. Describe how to use the Plan Review Tool to communicate the results of the review to a State or local community

C. Determine whether a Local Mitigation Plan meets Federal mitigation planning requirements

FEMA   Visual 3

Objectives:

At the end of this course, participants will be able to:

A. Explain the purpose and intent of reviewing Local Mitigation Plans

B. Describe how to use the Plan Review Tool to communicate the results of the review to a State or local community

C. Determine whether a Local mitigation plan meets Federal mitigation planning requirements

The intended audience for this course is new and experienced State and FEMA plan reviewers. FEMA plan reviewers may be full-time, FEMA Disaster Assistance Employees, or FEMA contract plan reviewers. The course is important because it discusses the purpose and intent of a plan review; how to recognize elements of plans that meet plan requirements; how to use the new Plan Review Tool; and how to convey the results of the review using the Regulation Checklist and the Plan Assessment parts of the Plan Review Tool.

This course addresses the review of Local Mitigation Plans only. It does not address review of plans prepared by State or Tribal governments.

Visual 4

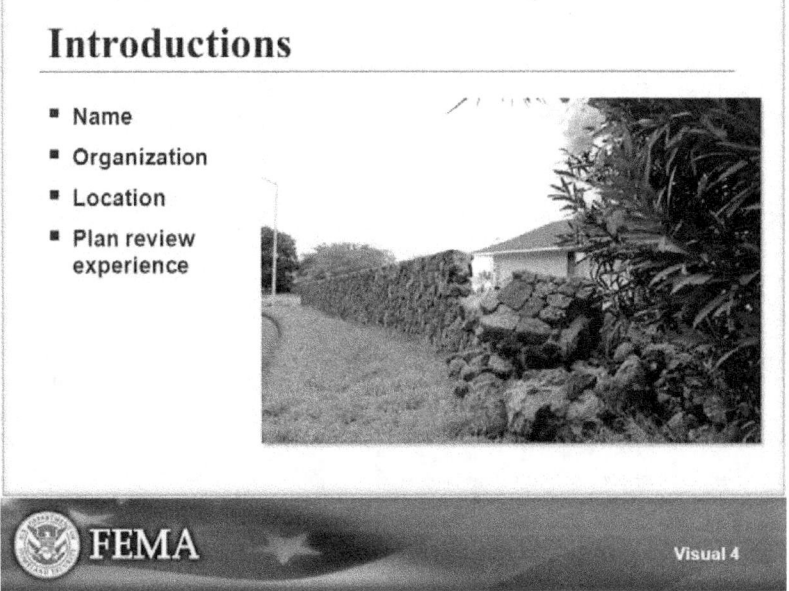

Introductions

- Name
- Organization
- Location
- Plan review experience

Please say your name, the name of the organization you are with, and the location of the organization, and indicate whether you have previously reviewed local hazard mitigation plans for FEMA.

 Photo shows earthquake damage in Hawaii.

Visual 5

Course Organization

1. Background
2. Guiding Principles
3. Overview of Plan Review Tool
4. Regulation Checklist
5. Plan Assessment
6. Wrap-Up and Post-Course Assessment

The course is organized in six sections.

1. The Background section describes the purpose of mitigation planning and the plan review process.

2. The second section explains each of the five Guiding Principles of FEMA's plan review.

3. The Overview of Plan Review Tool section introduces the purpose and organization of the Plan Review Tool.

4. The Regulation Checklist section provides details about the regulatory requirements for a Local Hazard Mitigation Plan. This is the longest of the five sections of the course.

5. The Plan Assessment section explains how to provide constructive feedback to a local community on the strengths of the plan, opportunities for improvement, and resources for

implementing the plan.

6. Finally, there will be a quick Wrap-up and quiz of key concepts discussed in the course to test your learning.

The estimated time to complete this training is 3 hours.

♪	Photo shows a mitigation display set up by FEMA.

Section 1. Background

Time: 20 minutes

OBJECTIVES

At the end of this section, participants will be able to:

- Describe the concepts critical for conducting plan reviews: mitigation planning, mitigation planning process, and roles of local communities, the State, and FEMA in reviewing a local mitigation plan

- Explain the purpose and intent of the mitigation plan review

METHODOLOGY

This section includes lecture and provides participants with the opportunity to ask questions.

Visual 6

1. Background

This section covers
- Hazard mitigation
- Hazard mitigation planning process
- Roles and responsibilities for plan review
- Legislative authority for plan review

FEMA   Visual 6

This section covers:

- Hazard mitigation
- Hazard mitigation planning process
- Roles and responsibilities for plan review
- Legislative authority for plan review

This section covers the purpose and intent of mitigation plan reviews. We will briefly cover what mitigation means, the mitigation planning process, Federal law that is the basis for planning requirements, and the roles of the local and State government and FEMA in mitigation plan reviews.

 Photo shows a street in Kentucky after a tornado.

Visual 7

Hazard Mitigation

- Reduces potential for
  - Loss of life
  - Injury
  - Property damage
- Sustained action
- Hazard mitigation actions
  - Implemented at any time
  - Based on an inclusive, comprehensive, long-term plan

 FEMA

Visual 7

- Reduces potential for:
  - Loss of life
  - Injury
  - Property damage
- Sustained action
- Hazard mitigation actions
  - Implemented at any time
  - Based on an inclusive, comprehensive, long-term plan

The purpose of hazard mitigation is to reduce potential losses from future hazards. Hazard mitigation actions reduce or eliminate the risk of loss of life, injury, and/or property damage and reduce the likelihood that a hazard will result in a disaster.

Local hazard mitigation strategies include land use policies and actions taken by communities to alter the built environment to build resiliency to natural hazards over time.

Hazard mitigation activities may be implemented at any time; communities need not wait until a disaster to consider taking actions that will reduce or eliminate the potential for damage. However, after a community experiences a disaster, rather than building back in the same way, the community can reduce the potential for future damage by mitigating risk as it repairs and rebuilds.

Decisions about the most appropriate hazard mitigation actions for a community should be made as a result of a thoughtful, diligent, inclusive, and comprehensive planning process. In this way, a community can institute a number of different hazard mitigation actions to build a more resilient community.

Note that not every natural hazard necessarily leads to a disaster. However, if natural hazards are severe and occur where people have developed structures and infrastructure, and if those structures and infrastructure cannot withstand the hazard, then a disaster may result.

Visual 8

Hazard Mitigation Planning Process

- Local Community
  - Develops a local mitigation plan
    - Involves the public and other stakeholders
    - Identifies and examines ALL potential natural hazards
    - Assesses vulnerabilities and impacts
    - Develops strategies to mitigate risks
  - Adopts the plan
  - Updates the plan
- No two communities are exactly alike; no two plans are exactly alike

FEMA   Visual 8

- Local Community
  - Develops a local mitigation plan
    - Involves the public and other stakeholders
    - Identifies and examines ALL potential natural hazards
    - Assesses vulnerabilities and impacts
    - Develops strategies to mitigate risks
  - Adopts the plan
  - Updates the plan
- No two communities are exactly alike; no two plans are exactly alike

To develop a mitigation plan, one or more local communities implement a planning process that utilizes the best available data and involves the public and the individuals in the community that have the authority and responsibility to work toward resiliency.

The local community identifies and examines each of the natural hazards that may cause damage in the community.

The local community conducts an assessment of risk and describes the potential impact of each hazard on the community.

Strategies or actions are proposed that address the risks

identified for each community.

Some plans represent a single jurisdiction; other plans are multi-jurisdictional. To demonstrate commitment to the mitigation plan and to implement the mitigation strategies, the plan is adopted by each local governing body.

Because conditions in a community change over time, the plan must be updated every 5 years to maintain eligibility for certain FEMA grant funds.

No two communities are exactly alike; therefore, no two plans should be identical. Communities have different geographies, patterns of development, types of development, political leadership, histories of damages and loss due to hazards, and so forth. There is no template for a hazard mitigation plan; plans may be formatted in the order of the regulations or following the regulation checklist, or in an order described through State guidance, or as part of another community plan (such as a comprehensive plan or emergency operations plan).

Visual 9

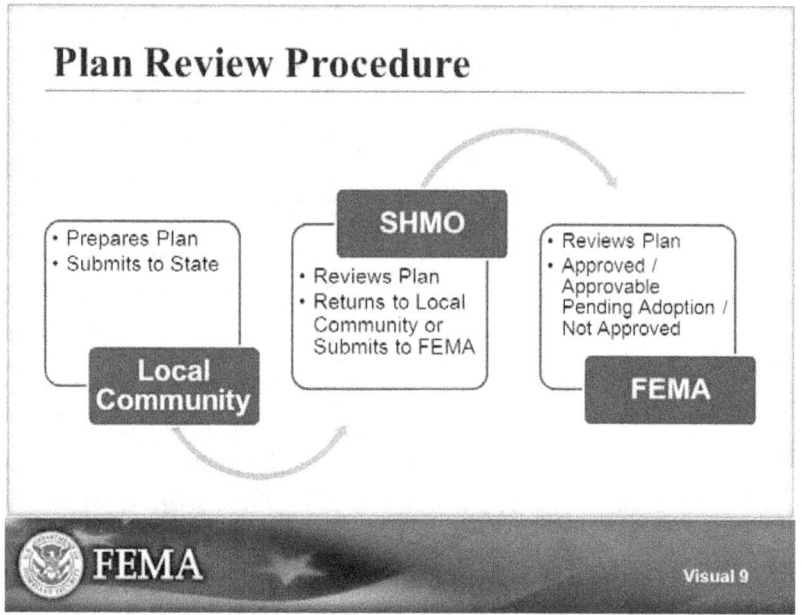

Local Community

- Prepares Plan
- Submits to State

SHMO

- Reviews Plan
- Returns to Local Community or Submits to FEMA

FEMA

- Reviews Plan
- Approved / Approvable Pending Adoption / Not Approved

After the local community prepares the plan, they do not submit the plan directly to FEMA. The local community submits the plan to the State Hazard Mitigation Officer (SHMO) for initial review.

The SHMO conducts the initial plan review to verify compliance with the Federal regulations. When the SHMO is confident that the plan is in compliance, the SHMO forwards the plan to the appropriate FEMA Regional Office for review.

The plan review will have one of three possible outcomes:

- Approved
- Approvable Pending Adoption, which means that

the plan must receive formal adoption by the local governing authority, such as the Board of Supervisors or the Town Council; when evidence of formal adoption is submitted to FEMA, the plan will be approved

- Not Approved, which means that the plan approvers have identified deficiencies; plan approvers use the Plan Review Tool, which will be discussed in detail in this presentation, to explain how the plan is not compliant with the regulations and to provide information about how to revise the plan so that it is compliant; the community will revise the plan accordingly and resubmit it to the SHMO

Visual 10

Procedural Notes

- Timing
- Communications
- Submittal
- Review and Revisions
- Approval and Adoption

FEMA   Visual 10

- Timing
- Communications
- Submittal
- Review and Revisions
- Approval and Adoption

Timing

FEMA plan reviewers complete the review of a local mitigation plan within 45 calendar days of receipt, whenever possible. If additional time is required, FEMA plan reviewers convey this information to the State as outlined in the Plan Review Guide. FEMA will work with State officials to prioritize the order in which plans are reviewed. If a FEMA review will not be completed within 45 days of receipt of the plan, FEMA will explain the cause of the delay to the State.

Communications

Communications about the plan are not limited to the Plan Review Tool. FEMA plan reviewers and State reviewers may discuss the plan or the review by phone or in person. States may include local officials in these discussions. When revisions to a plan are required, FEMA may contact the State by phone to discuss the revisions and offer an opportunity for changes to be made. The State may call FEMA for clarification about the findings of a review rather than conduct all communication in writing.

Submittal

The State can submit the plan to FEMA electronically or using a paper copy. The State may also submit a completed Plan Review Tool at the same time. If the Plan has already been adopted by one or more jurisdictions, the State will also send documentation of adoption. FEMA will provide confirmation of receipt to the State by phone, e-mail, or mail.

Review and Revisions

If a plan does not meet all of the requirements found in Title 44 of the Code of Federal Regulations (CFR) Section 201.6, the plan reviewer will use the Plan Review Tool to explain shortcomings and describe required revisions. The local community will revise and resubmit the plan to the State using the same process.

Approval and Adoption

When a plan meets the intent of the law and regulation, FEMA will send a letter confirming the "Approvable Pending Adoption" status of the plan and the State will communicate this to the local community.

The community has 1 calendar year from the date on the Approvable Pending Adoption letter to formally adopt the plan.

Usually, after a plan is deemed to be approvable pending adoption by FEMA, local communities formally adopt the plan and send documentation of adoption to the State, and the State forwards this to FEMA. At that point, FEMA will issue a formal letter of approval, which will indicate the expiration date of the plan.

Visual 11

Authority

Congress established requirements for mitigation plans

- Section 322 of the Robert T. Stafford Disaster Relief and Emergency Assistance Act (Stafford Act), as amended

- The National Flood Insurance Act of 1968 (NFIA), as amended

- Title 44 Code of Federal Regulations Section 201.6 (44 CFR 201.6)

FEMA   Visual 11

Congress established requirements for mitigation plans

- Section 322 of the Robert T. Stafford Disaster Relief and Emergency Assistance Act (Stafford Act), as amended

- The National Flood Insurance Act of 1968 (NFIA), as amended

- Title 44 Code of Federal Regulations Section 201.6 (44 CFR 201.6)

The Stafford Act constitutes the statutory authority for most Federal disaster response activities, especially as they pertain to FEMA and FEMA programs. It gives FEMA its authority to establish regulations and administer the law. Congress amended the Stafford Act in 2000 and established a process for providing pre-disaster and post-disaster funds to mitigate risks to reduce the degree to which future natural hazards would lead to disasters.

In addition, the National Flood Insurance Program (NFIP) has programs that provide grants to local communities to mitigate flood risks.

To be eligible for certain pre-disaster funds, whether established by the Stafford Act or the NFIP, a local community must have a FEMA-approved mitigation plan.

The specific local hazard mitigation plan regulations that implement the Stafford Act are found in 44 CFR 201.6. Each plan is reviewed to establish compliance with these

Federal requirements. This training will cover these plan requirements and how they are interpreted in the Plan Review Guide.

Despite some modification in the approach used for conducting a review of a local hazard mitigation plan, the law and the requirements specified in 44 CFR 201.6 have not changed. Nevertheless, some changes have been made in the plan review guidance.

The Stafford Act as amended in 2000 is often referred to as the Disaster Mitigation Act of 2000.

Visual 12

Questions?

- The Background section provided information about:
  - Hazard mitigation
  - Mitigation planning process
  - Legislative authority
  - Roles and responsibilities of local communities, State, or FEMA
- Questions?

FEMA   Visual 12

- The Background section provided information about:

  o Hazard mitigation

  o Mitigation planning process

  o Legislative authority

  o Roles and responsibilities of local communities, State, or FEMA

Questions?

Each of the concepts presented in this section is critical to conducting a plan review. This section provided the background for mitigation planning and the mitigation planning process. We also addressed legislative authority and the roles of local communities, the State, and FEMA in reviewing a local mitigation plan. In particular, this section addressed the first objective of the course and participants should now understand the purpose and intent of the mitigation plan review.

Are there any questions?

 Photo shows hurricane shutters on elevated structure in North Carolina.

Section 2. Guiding Principles

Time: 20 minutes

OBJECTIVES

At the end of this unit, participants will be able to:

- Describe the Guiding Principles that are important to keep in mind while doing a plan review to ensure that reviews are fair and reasonable

METHODOLOGY

This unit includes lecture and provides participants with the opportunity to ask questions.

Visual 13

2. Guiding Principles

- This section covers the five Guiding Principles for plan reviewers
  - Guiding Principle #1: Focus on the mitigation strategy
  - Guiding Principle #2: Review for intent as well as compliance
  - Guiding Principle #3: Understand that the process is as important as the plan itself
  - Guiding Principle #4: Understand that this is the community's plan
  - Guiding Principle #5: Use the plan review to foster relationships

 FEMA

Visual 13

Guiding Principles

This section covers the five Guiding Principles for plan reviewers

- Guiding Principle #1: Focus on the mitigation strategy

- Guiding Principle #2: Review for intent as well as compliance

- Guiding Principle #3: Understand that the process is as important as the plan itself

- Guiding Principle #4: Understand that this is the community's plan

- Guiding Principle #5: Use the plan review to foster relationships

This section presents the Five Guiding Principles for plan reviewers, as described in the Plan Review Guide.

The Guiding Principles are important and plan reviewers should keep them in mind while conducting a plan review. The Guiding Principles provide a basic check for plan reviewers to ensure that reviews are fair and reasonable. If a plan reviewer is in doubt about whether a specific requirement has been met, he or she should revisit these Guiding Principles to validate whether the basic intent is being met.

Visual 14

Guiding Principle #1

Focus on the mitigation strategy.

- Emphasize actions and implementation
- Purpose of the planning process is to develop a sound mitigation strategy that will be effective in reducing losses

First, emphasize the plan review on the mitigation actions and implementation of the mitigation strategy.

The actual purpose of the planning process and risk assessment is to develop a sound, rational, and reasonable mitigation strategy that will be implemented to reduce damage and losses. Thus, plan reviewers will focus on the mitigation strategy or the actions that a community proposes for implementation.

 Photo shows a public building in Louisiana elevated to mitigate future flood and storm surge damage.

Visual 15

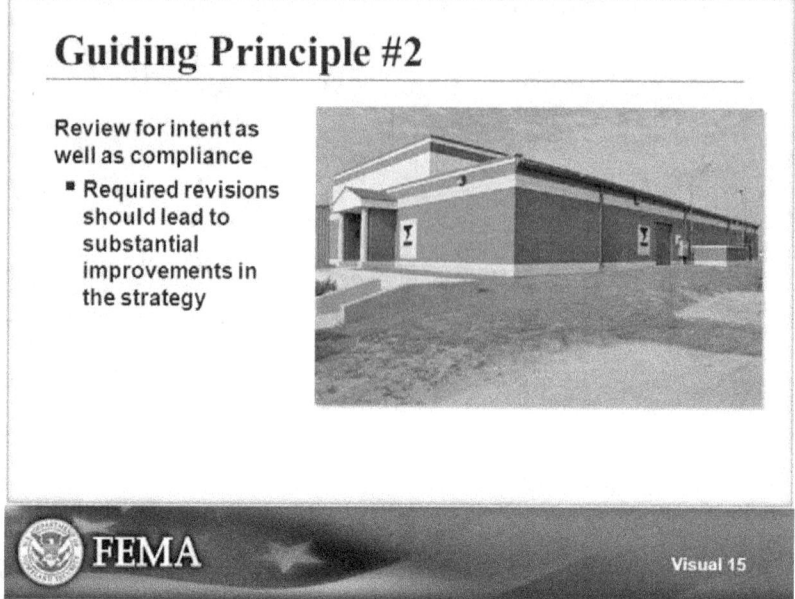

Guiding Principle #2

Review for intent as well as compliance.

- Required revisions should lead to substantial improvements in the strategy

Second, a strict interpretation of the individual requirements of Federal mitigation planning regulations may lead communities to spend resources to make revisions that do not substantially improve the mitigation strategy. Plan reviewers will review the plan for intent of the regulation as well as for compliance with regulations.

 Photo shows a community safe room built in Oklahoma to protect people from tornadoes.

Visual 16

Guiding Principle # 3

Understand that the process of developing a local hazard mitigation plan is as important as the plan itself.

- Process is not defined by FEMA

- Process is defined locally

Third, each community has developed traditions and has learned how best to conduct planning locally. Plan reviewers will accept the planning process as defined by the community. Federal regulations state that the plan must describe the planning process that was implemented; Federal regulations do not specify HOW the process must be conducted.

	Photo shows a community planning meeting in New York.

Visual 17

Guiding Principle #4

Understand that this is the community's plan

- FEMA does not require that plans have a particular organization

FEMA   Visual 17

Guiding Principle # 4

Understand that this is the community's plan.

- FEMA does not require that plans have a particular organization

Fourth, the mitigation plan is the community's plan. Plan reviewers will not require that plans be organized using a specific format.

Similarly, FEMA does not require that specific types of projects be proposed for implementation.

 Photo shows a structure that a community in Louisiana has acquired and is demolishing to prevent future flood damages.

Visual 18

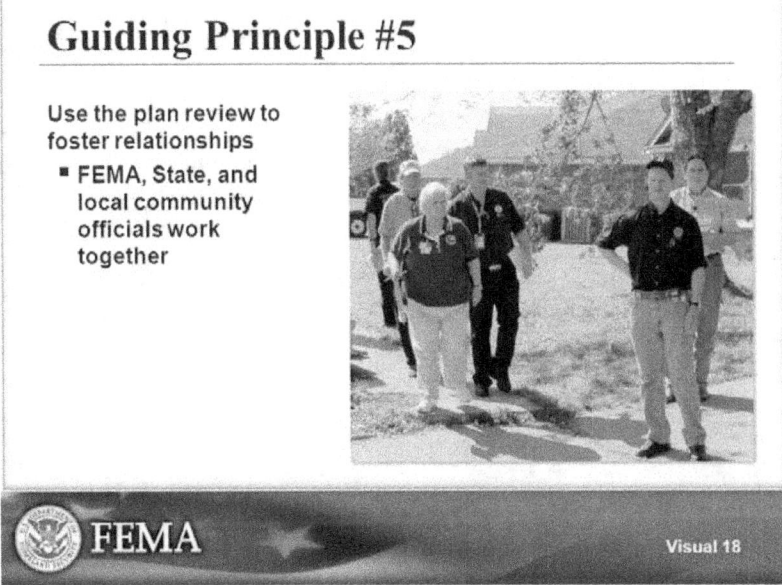

Guiding Principle # 5

Use the plan review to foster relationships.

- FEMA, State, and local community officials work together

Plan Reviewers understand that the plan is not a one-time effort; the relationship between FEMA and the States and local communities is an important working relationship. The role of Plan Reviewers is to provide technical assistance that will facilitate the development of mitigation plans and enhance the plans, not to be gatekeepers of plan approval and to threaten working relationships.

 Photo shows FEMA and local officials working together in Texas in the aftermath of a disaster.

Visual 19

FEMA Approach

- The FEMA approach to mitigation planning is performance based and identifies generally what should happen and what should be documented in the plan

- The FEMA approach is not prescriptive and does not specify exactly how the planning process should be conducted.

FEMA   Visual 19

- The FEMA approach to mitigation planning is performance based and identifies generally what should happen and what should be documented in the plan

- The FEMA approach is not prescriptive and does not specify exactly how the planning process should be conducted.

Visual 20

Questions?

- Focus on the mitigation strategy
- Review for intent as well as compliance
- Understand that the process is as important as the plan itself
- Understand that this is the community's plan
- Use the plan review to foster relationships
- Questions?

FEMA   Visual 20

Questions?

- Focus on the mitigation strategy

- Review for intent as well as compliance

- Understand that the process is as important as the plan itself

- Understand that this is the community's plan

- Use the plan review to foster relationships

- Questions?

This section introduced the five Guiding Principles for plan approvers.

The principles are to focus on the strategy, review for intent as well as compliance, understand that the process and the actual plan are as unique as each community, and to understand that the plan review provides an opportunity to foster relationships among local, State, and Federal government entities. This section addressed the second course objective and participants should now understand how to approach the review.

Are there any questions?

Section 3. Overview of Plan Review Resources

Time: 30 minutes

OBJECTIVES

At the end of this unit, participants will be able to:

- Describe the content of the Plan Review Tool
- Describe how to use the Plan Review tool

METHODOLOGY

This unit includes lecture and provides participants with the opportunity to ask questions.

Visual 21

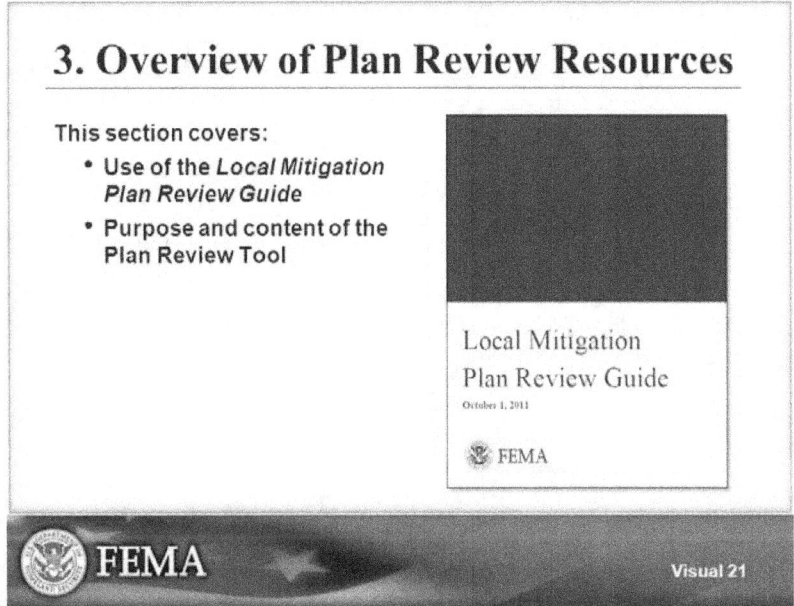

3. Overview of Plan Review Resources

This section covers:

- Use of the FEMA 2011 *Local Mitigation Plan Review Guide*

- Purpose and content of the Plan Review Tool

This section covers the *Local Mitigation Plan Review Guide* and the purpose and content of Appendix A, the Plan Review Tool.

Visual 22

Local Mitigation Plan Review Guide

- FEMA's official interpretation of 44 CFR 201.6
- FEMA's standard operating procedure for review of a Local Mitigation Plan
- Must be consulted by FEMA plan approvers when reviewing a Local Mitigation Plan

The *Local Mitigation Plan Review Guide* is the official source of information about the review of local hazard mitigation plans. Many workshops and guidebooks have been developed since the Disaster Mitigation Act became law in 2000.

The Plan Review Guide provides information relative to both the first plan as well as to any updated plan that a community may submit for review.

The Plan Review Guide represents the FEMA interpretation of Federal regulations, includes references to specific language in 44 CFR 201.6, and presents a standard procedure to be used nationwide so that plan review is consistent across the 10 FEMA Regions.

The Plan Review Guide must be consulted by FEMA plan approvers when reviewing a Local Mitigation Plan.

Visual 23

Plan Review Tool

- The Local Mitigation Plan Review Tool is Appendix A of the Plan Review Guide
- Plan reviewers use the Local Mitigation Plan Review Tool to:
  - Demonstrate how the plan meets the regulations in 44 CFR 201.6
  - Provide feedback to the community
- The Tool has four parts
  - Cover Page
  - Regulation Checklist
  - Plan Assessment
  - Multi-jurisdiction Summary Sheet

 FEMA   Visual 23

Plan Review Tool

- The Local Mitigation Plan Review Tool is Appendix A of the Plan Review Guide

- Plan reviewers use the Local Mitigation Plan Review Tool to:

  - Demonstrate how the plan meets the regulations in 44 CFR 201.6

  - Provide feedback to the community

- The Tool has four parts

  - Cover Page

  - Regulation Checklist

  - Plan Assessment

  - Multi-jurisdiction Summary Sheet

The Tool is an Appendix to the Plan Review Guide.

The Tool is used by FEMA plan reviewers to record whether a plan has met the legal requirements. It is also a document used to communicate feedback to local communities.

The Tool has four parts, which will be discussed in detail during this presentation.

Visual 24

Cover Page

- Includes Local Mitigation Plan information
- Dates of State and FEMA review
- Determination of review

The first part of the Tool is the Cover Page, which is found on page A-1. The Cover Page provides space for the local community to list the jurisdiction(s) represented, the title, and date of the plan. The community should also provide contact information for the main point of contact associated with the plan.

The Cover Page also includes a box for the State to record the date of their review.

Finally, FEMA has boxes to record the dates of the submittal and the review decision.

Image shows the cover page of the Plan Review Tool.

Visual 25

Regulation Checklist

- Lists all Federal requirements that use the verb "shall"
- Leads the plan reviewer through systematic consideration of each required element, with definitions and examples
- Allows for additional State requirements

Visual 25

Regulation Checklist

- Lists all Federal requirements that use the verb "shall"

- Leads the plan reviewer through systematic consideration of each required element, with definitions and examples

- Allows for additional State requirements

The main body of the Plan Review Tool is the Regulation Checklist, which is found on pages A-2 through A-4.

The Regulation Checklist includes only the Federal hazard mitigation plan requirements that are stated using the verb "shall" in 44 CFR Part 201.6. The CFR language is included in the black boxes throughout Section 4 of the Plan Review Guide.

The Regulation Checklist guides the plan reviewer so that each requirement is considered. Plan reviewers indicate the location in the plan where the requirement has been addressed and indicate that the plan has either met or has not met the requirement. If the plan has not met the intent of the requirement, the plan reviewer must identify which sub-element has not been met.

The plan reviewer must include a succinct, precise explanation of the plan's shortcomings along with a description of required revisions in the "Required Revisions" box under the corresponding element.

The Plan Review Guide explains how the requirements are interpreted by FEMA and includes examples of one or more approaches to meeting each requirement. Examples are not inclusive of all possible solutions to meet a requirement, and they are not necessarily considered best practices or exemplary examples.

 Photo shows an irrigation canal in California that was damaged by an earthquake.

Visual 26

Plan Assessment

- To offer more comprehensive feedback on the quality of the plan to the local community
  - Suggestions for improving the Plan
  - Strengths of the Plan
  - Recommendations for implementation
- Lists regulations that use the verb "should"
- FEMA plan approvers must complete the Plan Assessment

FEMA   Visual 26

Plan Assessment

- To offer more comprehensive feedback on the quality of the plan to the local community

  o Suggestions for improving the Plan

  o Strengths of the Plan

  o Recommendations for implementation

- Lists regulations that use the verb "should"

- FEMA plan approvers must complete the Plan Assessment

The third part of the Plan Review Tool is the Plan Assessment, which is found on pages A-5 through A-8.

This section of the Plan Review Tool provides space for the plan approver to provide suggestions for improving the plan, comments on the quality or strengths of the plan, recommendations or opportunities for implementing the plan, or other information that might be useful.

The Plan Assessment lists FEMA recommendations for a good hazard mitigation plan, which are found in 44 CFR 201.6 and use the verb "should." These are not required but may provide good suggestions for revisions to the plan now or as part of the next plan update.

FEMA plan approvers must complete appropriate sections of the Plan Assessment. State reviewers may complete this section as well, because they often have the greater understanding of the local community capabilities.

Visual 27

Multi-jurisdiction Summary Sheet

- Optional
- List each of the jurisdictions
  - Enter contact information
  - Keep track of which requirements were "Met" or "Not Met" for each jurisdiction
- Plan reviewers cannot approve a plan unless each requirement is met for each participating jurisdiction

Multi-jurisdiction Summary Sheet

- Optional

- List each of the jurisdictions

  o Enter contact information

  o Keep track of which requirements were "Met" or "Not Met" for each jurisdiction

- Plan reviewers cannot approve a plan unless each requirement is met for each participating jurisdiction

The fourth part of the Tool is the Multi-jurisdiction Summary Sheet. This part is included for convenience and is optional.

It may be used to list the names of the jurisdictions covered by the plan as well as contact information. This information should be completed by the local community as part of their submittal to the State.

It provides space for recording, by jurisdiction, whether the requirements were met or not met.

This may serve as a reminder and tracking device for the plan preparer as well as the plan reviewer to ensure that each jurisdiction seeking plan approval has in fact engaged in the planning process, assessed their unique risks and vulnerabilities, identified mitigation actions for which they are responsible, identified a community-tailored approach to plan implementation and maintenance, and adopted the plan.

The plan cannot be approved by the plan reviewer unless each requirement is met for each participating jurisdiction.

Visual 28

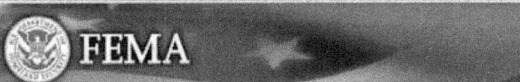

Questions?

- This section provided an overview of:
  - The *Local Mitigation Plan Review Guide*
  - The Plan Review Tool
    - Cover Page
    - Regulation Checklist
    - Plan Assessment
    - Multi-jurisdiction Summary Sheet (optional)
- Questions?

FEMA   Visual 28

Questions?

- This section provided an overview of:
  - The *Local Mitigation Plan Review Guide*
  - The Plan Review Tool
    - Cover Page
    - Regulation Checklist
    - Plan Assessment
    - Multi-jurisdiction Summary Sheet (optional)
- Questions?

This section provided an overview of the Plan Review Guide and the four sections of the Plan Review Tool: the Cover Page, the Regulation Checklist, the Plan Assessment, and the Multi-jurisdiction Summary Sheet. The remainder of the course examines the Regulation Checklist and Plan Assessment in greater depth.

Are there any questions?

 Photo shows debris along a street in New York after a flood.

Section 4. Regulation Checklist

Time: 30 minutes

OBJECTIVES

At the end of this unit, participants will be able to:

- Describe how to recognize elements of plans that meet plan requirements
- Describe how to convey the results of the review using the Regulation Checklist

METHODOLOGY

This unit includes lecture and provides opportunity to participants for asking questions.

Visual 29

4. Regulation Checklist

Regulation Checklist has 6 Elements

A. Planning Process

B. Hazard Identification and Risk Assessment

C. Mitigation Strategy

D. Plan Review, Evaluation, and Implementation (for plan updates only)

E. Plan Adoption

F. Additional State Requirements (for State reviewers only)

The Regulation Checklist has 6 elements.

For every plan, the FEMA plan approver will examine:

- Element A: Planning Process

- Element B: Hazard Identification and Risk Assessment

- Element C: Mitigation Strategy

- Element E: Plan Adoption

If a community has had an approved hazard mitigation plan in the past and the plan being reviewed is an update, then the plan review includes:

- Element D: Plan Review, Evaluation, and Implementation

Some States have additional requirements. State reviewers review these requirements and use:

- Element F: Additional State Requirements

The key points are pulled out for each element, but for the comprehensive interpretation refer to the Plan Review Guide.

Visual 30

Element A. Planning Process

- Intent of Element A
  - Planning process is appropriate for the community
  - Plan provides a permanent record of how decisions were reached
- An open public involvement process is required

FEMA   Visual 30

Element A. Planning Process

- Intent of Element A

  - Planning process is appropriate for the community

  - Plan provides a permanent record of how decisions were reached

- An open public involvement process is required

Element A concerns the planning process. The regulations state that an open public involvement process is essential to the development of an effective plan. Remember the Guiding Principle that the planning process is as important as the plan itself.

By involving the public, a broad range of perspectives will be considered relative to the characteristics and potential impacts of hazards and the range of potential solutions. The plan must not be a research paper about natural hazards; the focus of the plan must be on developing a community-derived mitigation strategy that is based on the financial, technical, and human resources of a community.

Local leadership and staffing fluctuate over time, and institutional knowledge of how the mitigation plan was developed will be lost. Thus, the plan must contain a permanent record of how decisions were reached and who was involved in reaching mitigation decisions.

FEMA will accept the planning process as defined by the community; but the plan must include a narrative description and documentation of the process for all new or updated plans.

Photo shows a fishing boat used in Alaska to deliver supplies to a village.

Participants should follow the Regulations Checklist section of the Plan Review Guide for this part of the course.

Visual 31

A1. Document the Planning Process

- How was the plan developed?
  - Schedule and summary of activities
- Who was involved in the process for each jurisdiction?
  - Names or titles of agencies involved
  - Copies of meeting agendas
  - Sign-in sheets
- How was the public engaged in the process?
  - Applies to new plans and plan updates
  - Questionnaires, surveys
  - Integration of feedback into the plan

 FEMA

Visual 31

A1. Document the Planning Process

- How was the plan developed?
  - Schedule and summary of activities
- Who was involved in the process for each jurisdiction?
  - Names or titles of agencies involved
  - Copies of meeting agendas
  - Sign-in sheets
- How was the public engaged in the process?
  - Applies to new plans and plan updates
  - Questionnaires, surveys
  - Integration of feedback into the plan

Involvement in the process means having the chance to affect the content of the plan.

The plan must provide information about a public involvement process whether it is the first plan developed by a community or an update of a previous mitigation plan. Plan reviewers look for information about who was involved in the planning process for each jurisdiction.

Plan reviewers look for documentation of public involvement in the plan such as:

- A narrative description of the process

- Copies of meeting agendas or minutes and sign-in sheets

- Copies of newspaper, web postings, radio or television announcements about the planning process

- Copies of meeting announcements or letters of invitation

- Questionnaires or surveys

- Opportunities for the public to discuss the plan with plan developers at community events

- A narrative description is sufficient to meet this requirement, and meeting notes, sign-in sheets, etc., are not required as long as there is enough information to describe the process (again, the who, when, where, when). These examples (meeting notes, sign-in sheets, etc.) are provided to show alternative ways to meet the requirement if the community simply wants to reference these as their record of the planning process.

Visual 32

A2. Stakeholder Engagement

- An opportunity for broad involvement is required

- Does the plan identify stakeholders given an opportunity to be involved?

- Opportunity for involvement must be provided for

  - Local and regional agencies involved in mitigation

  - Agencies with the authority to regulate development

  - Neighboring communities

The intent of this regulation is that the plan demonstrates that the process provided opportunities for a broad range of stakeholders to be involved. Such stakeholders might provide additional data or expertise needed to develop the plan, have knowledge of regional hazard mitigation efforts, or be affected by mitigation measures.

Plan reviewers look for information about efforts to involve the following types of stakeholders:

- Agencies involved in hazard mitigation or planning, such as public works, zoning, emergency management, floodplain administration, special districts, and GIS

- Agencies with authority to regulate development, such as planning and community development departments, building officials, planning commissions, and elected officials

- Neighboring communities, counties, municipalities, reservations, and so forth that are affected by similar hazard events

Local and regional agencies involved in mitigation, agencies with the authority to regulate development, and neighboring communities may be given the opportunity to participate. Other stakeholders are defined by each jurisdiction and could include representatives of the business, academic, and non-profit sectors depending on the unique characteristics of the community.

Visual 33

A3. Opportunity for Public Involvement

Does the Plan:

- Document opportunities for the public to be involved during the drafting stage?

- Explain how public feedback was incorporated into the plan?

Note that the drafting stage occurs during plan development and prior to the formal comment period on the plan just before plan adoption.

Plan reviewers look for documentation of opportunities for the public to be involved during the drafting stage.

Plan reviewers also look for information about how public comments were incorporated into or affected the plan.

 Photo shows a public open-house meeting held in Louisiana.

Visual 34

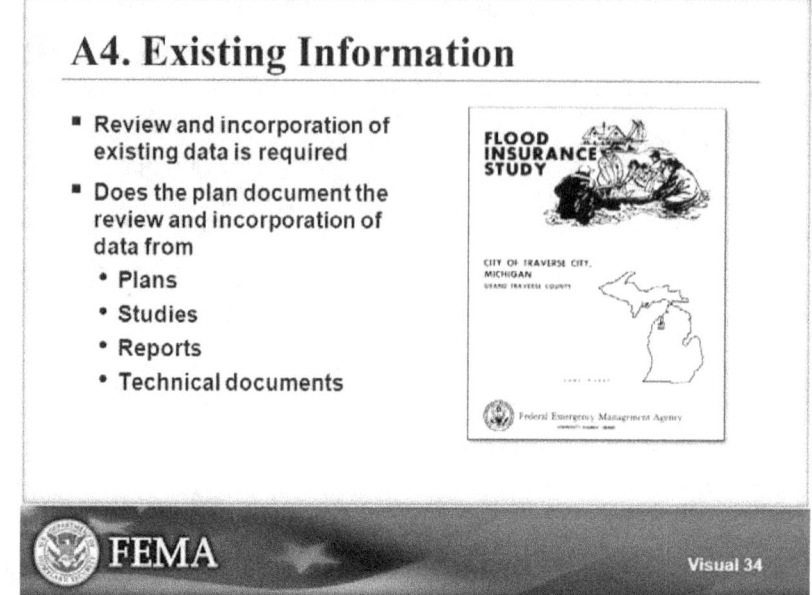

A4. Existing Information

- Review and incorporation of existing data is required

- Does the plan document the review and incorporation of data from

    o Plans

    o Studies

    o Reports

    o Technical documents

The plan must explain what existing documents or studies were reviewed to gather information about hazards or community vulnerabilities. Examples of sources of existing data include the State hazard mitigation plan, the local comprehensive plan, a flood insurance study, stormwater management plan, capital improvement plan, sustainability plan, or zoning map.

The plan may include a list of references, include footnotes, etc., or may include a list of plans and studies that were incorporated into the plan. Plan reviewers should also look for information about how relevant information was incorporated into the mitigation plan.

For example, a local comprehensive plan may identify the need for additional space for outdoor recreation as a result of population growth and list as a goal: "Establish additional outdoor recreational areas." The hazard mitigation plan could recommend acquisition of properties in the floodplain as a mitigation action. The hazard mitigation plan could cite the goal from the comprehensive plan and show that property acquisition is an opportunity for the establishment of additional outdoor recreational areas.

If a plan contains no information about existing data that contribute to an understanding of hazards or vulnerabilities, plan reviewers may look for recognition of the need for additional data and a corresponding mitigation action for conducting future research to enhance the understanding of hazards and vulnerabilities in the planning area. Plan reviewers may also move to the Plan Assessment section of the Tool and recommend that the plan clearly state that there are no existing sources of local data and suggest that the applicable State hazard mitigation plan would be a good reference document.

Visual 35

A5. Continued Public Participation

- Continued public participation is required
- Does the plan describe how jurisdiction(s) will seek public participation
  - After plan adoption?
  - During implementation, monitoring, and evaluation?

A5. Continued Public Participation

- Continued public participation is required

- Does the plan describe how jurisdiction(s) will seek public participation

  - After plan adoption?

  - During implementation, monitoring, and evaluation?

As mitigation strategies are implemented and as conditions in the community change, the plan is regularly evaluated to determine if it is up-to-date. Even if no hazards affect the community and conditions are relatively stable, social, financial, and political support to implement mitigation actions can change over time.

Plan reviewers look for evidence that each participating community will provide opportunities for public participation during plan implementation, such as periodic presentations on the plan's status to their elected officials or community groups, annual questionnaires or surveys, public meetings, and interactive Web site information about plan implementation.

♪ Photo shows public participatory event in Alabama.

Visual 36

A6. Keeping the Plan Current

- A method and schedule for keeping the plan current is required
- Does the plan identify how, when, and by whom it will be:
  - Monitored?
  - Evaluated?
  - Updated?

 FEMA   Visual 36

A6. Keeping the Plan Current

- A method and schedule for keeping the plan current is required

- Does the plan identify how, when, and by whom it will be:

  - Monitored?

  - Evaluated?

  - Updated?

Plan reviewers look for information about how, when, and by whom the plan will be monitored, evaluated, and updated.

Monitoring means tracking the implementation of the plan over time.

- Plan reviewers ask: Does the plan describe how the implementation of the hazard mitigation actions will be tracked?

Evaluating means assessing the effectiveness of the plan at achieving its stated purpose and goals.

- Plan reviewers ask: Does the plan describe how the community will regularly assess the effectiveness of the plan in achieving its stated purpose and goals?

Updating means reviewing and revising the plan at least once every 5 years.

- Plan reviewers ask: Does the plan describe how, when, and by whom the plan will be updated?

- Plan reviewers ask: Does the plan include the title of the individual or name of the department/agency responsible for leading each of these efforts?

Plan reviewers look for an indication of how each of these activities will be carried out, when each will be initiated, and the position or department that will be responsible for leading the monitoring, evaluation, and updating efforts.

Visual 37

Element B: Hazard Identification and Risk Assessment

- The plan must describe potential hazards

- Intent of Element B

    o Use of accurate, current, and relevant information

    o Basis for assessing vulnerability

    o Leads to mitigation strategy

Element B is about identification of hazards and assessing the risk posed by each identified hazard.

Remember the Guiding Principle that the plan review should "focus on the mitigation strategy." The purpose of the risk assessment is to develop a sound, relevant mitigation strategy with proposed mitigation actions that address each community's unique vulnerabilities. The risk assessment provides a justification for spending community resources to implement hazard mitigation measures.

Visual 38

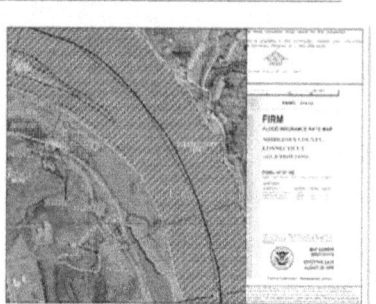

B1. Type, Location, and Extent

- Description of natural hazards is required

- Description of location and extent is required

- Does the plan
  - Describe potential natural hazards?
  - Provide rationale for omitting a natural hazard?
  - Explain location and extent of each potential natural hazard?

FEMA   Visual 38

B1. Type, Location, and Extent

- Description of natural hazards is required

- Description of location and extent is required

- Does the plan:

  - Describe potential natural hazards?

  - Provide rationale for omitting a natural hazard?

  - Explain location and extent of each potential natural hazard?

The plan must describe natural hazards that can affect the entire planning area, as well as hazards that affect only some locations in the planning area. A multi-jurisdictional plan must describe natural hazards that can affect all of the jurisdictions participating in the plan, as well as those that only affect some of the participating jurisdictions. For example, a plan from a coastal county may describe coastal storm surge as a hazard affecting only those jurisdictions located along the coast.

If a hazard that is commonly thought to be possible in the planning area is omitted from the plan, the plan reviewers look for an explanation of why that particular hazard has been omitted.

Plan reviewers should review data about types, locations, and extents of hazards to determine whether the plan indicates that the community has developed an understanding of the hazards that can occur in the planning area.

For each hazard, plan reviewers look for information about the locations where they can occur. Location means the geographic areas that can be affected by a particular hazard. For many hazards, such as flooding or landslide, maps can be used to illustrate location; however, location may be described in a narrative.

If a hazard such as tornadoes, extreme heat, severe winter storms, or high winds can affect the entire planning area, plan reviewers may find explicit statements to the effect that the location of such hazards is the entire planning area or may understand that the plan implies that these hazards can affect the entire planning area.

For each identified hazard, plan reviewers look for information about the potential extent or magnitude of each hazard. Extent means the strength or magnitude of a particular hazard. Extent can be described in terms of a scientific scale such as the Enhanced Fujita Scale, Saffir-Simpson Hurricane Scale, Richter Scale, or flood-depth grids. Extent could be explained by the duration of a hazard and/or the speed of onset. Note that extent is not the same as location or "impact."

Image shows a FIRMETTE for part of the Special Flood Hazard Area along the Connecticut River; the floodway is depicted by stripes and the Zone AE floodplain by aqua dots.

Visual 39

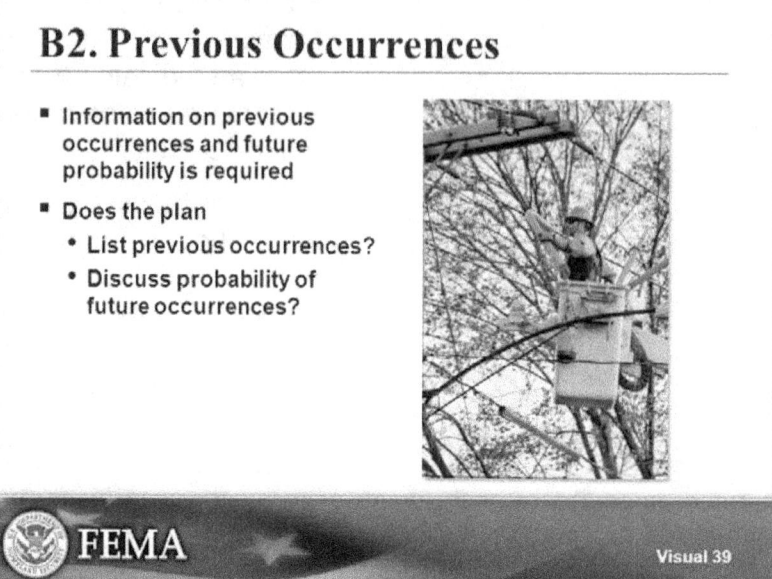

B2. Previous Occurrences

- Information on previous occurrences and future probability is required

- Does the plan

  o List previous occurrences?

  o Discuss probability of future occurrences?

Plan reviewers look for information in the plan about previous occurrences of each identified natural hazard. The number and dates of previous occurrences are the sample data that can be used to develop an estimate of the probability or likelihood of that hazard occurring in the future.

Probability may be described using terms such as highly likely, likely, and unlikely. However, if general descriptors are used, plan reviewers look for definitions of the terms in the plan.

Information about probability may also be included in the plan through inclusion of a probability map showing hazard probabilities.

Plan updates must include occurrences since the previous plan was approved.

♪ Photo shows tree limbs being cut in Connecticut after a high wind event.

Visual 40

B3. Impact and Vulnerability

- Description of impact and vulnerability is required
- Does the plan
  - Describe potential impacts?
  - Describe assets such as
    - People?
    - Structures?
    - Facilities?
    - Systems?
    - Capabilities?
    - Activities?
  - Summarize vulnerabilities?
    - Issues or problems

Visual 40

B3. Impact and Vulnerability

- Description of impact and vulnerability is required
- Does the plan
  - o Describe potential impacts?
  - o Describe assets such as
    - – People?
    - – Structures?
    - – Facilities?
    - – Systems?
    - – Capabilities?
    - – Activities?
  - o Summarize vulnerabilities?
    - – Issues or problems

For each participating jurisdiction, plan reviewers look for a description of the potential impacts of each hazard. Impact means the consequence or effects of the hazard on people, structures, facilities, systems, capabilities, or activities. Potential impacts might be based on previous impacts of hazards in the community.

Examples of impacts are damaged residential, commercial, and public structures; damaged utility lines and roads; loss of power; the need for rescue services and emergency shelters; damage to an environmental or cultural asset; and temporary loss of jobs. Impacts vary by community.

Plan reviewers look for a summary of each jurisdiction's vulnerability. The summary identifies people, structures, or systems that are susceptible to damage or loss. For example, the plan might state that there is one school in the inundation area that might be affected by dam failure; that there are two restaurants in a floodway; that there are dozens of homes and businesses in a floodplain; that there is a large parking lot built over an area that is prone to subsidence; that there are hundreds of homes scattered throughout an area that is vulnerable to wildfire; and that there are hundreds of structures in the community that were built before building codes were adopted and that might be damaged by an earthquake. An overall summary can be a list of key issues or problem statements that clearly describe the vulnerabilities that will be addressed in the mitigation strategy.

Photo shows flood damage to a covered bridge in Vermont.

Visual 41

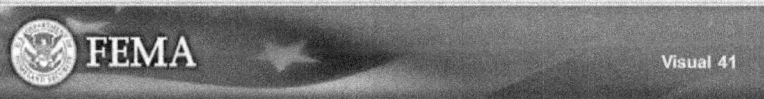

B4. NFIP-Insured Structures

- Information about repetitively flooded NFIP-insured structures is required
- Does the plan
  - Describe types of structures?
  - Estimate number of repetitive loss properties?
  - Not violate conditions of Privacy Act of 1974?

FEMA   Visual 41

B4. NFIP-Insured Structures

- Information about repetitively flooded NFIP-insured structures is required

- Does the plan

  - Describe types of structures?

  - Estimate number of repetitive loss properties?

  - Not violate conditions of Privacy Act of 1974?

To further develop an understanding of vulnerability to flood damage, plans must include information about the types and numbers of repetitive loss (RL) or severe repetitive loss (SRL) properties in each jurisdiction in the planning area. Note that FEMA has defined "Repetitive Loss" properties as having had two or more losses with at least $1,000 payments from the NFIP within any 10-year period since 1978 and "Severe Repetitive Loss" properties as having had at least four NFIP payments of over $5,000 totaling more than $20,000 or at least two separate NFIP payments with the cumulative amount exceeding the market value of the building. FEMA plan reviewers can verify this information using BureauNet. If jurisdictions do not have RL or SRL properties, plan reviewers look for a statement that the jurisdictions have no RL or SRL properties.

Plans must not release the names of NFIP policy holders or amounts of claims payments; that would be a violation of the Privacy Act of 1974. If plan reviewers find such information in the plan, the plan cannot be approved until it is removed.

 Photo shows a Louisiana home being elevated.

Visual 42

Additional Notes

- FEMA does not require a specific format for the plan
- The Regulation Checklist only includes requirements of 44 CFR 201.6 that use the words "shall" or "must"
- Leadership in local government may fluctuate over time; therefore, describing the process and explaining how decisions were reached is important

FEMA   Visual 42

Present the following points and ask participants if they have questions.

- Additional notes

  o FEMA does not require specific formats for the plan

  o The Regulation Checklist only includes requirements of 44 CFR 201.6 that use the words "shall" and "must"

  o Leadership in local government may fluctuate over time; therefore, explaining how decisions were reached is important

- Are there any questions?

 Each note is based on information found on pages 13 and 14 of the FEMA 2011 *Local Mitigation Plan Review Guide*.

Visual 43

Element C. Mitigation Strategy

- The plan must include a mitigation strategy
  - o A blueprint for reducing potential losses
  - o Based on existing policies, programs, resources
- Intent of Element C
  - o Describe hazard mitigation goals and actions
  - o Identify the community's existing authorities, policies, programs, and resources that can be used to implement those actions
  - o All other requirements lead to and support the mitigation strategy
  - o Mitigation actions must be reaffirmed or updated when the plan is updated

The Stafford Act requires that Local Mitigation Plans describe hazard mitigation actions and establish a strategy for implementing those actions. All other requirements for a Local Mitigation Plan lead to the development of the mitigation strategy.

The mitigation strategy includes the development of goals and prioritized hazard mitigation actions or projects for each participating jurisdiction. It should be a blueprint based on existing community policies and resources and should build on existing community capabilities.

Note that in a plan update, the strategy is either reaffirmed or updated based on current conditions. Current conditions include the completion of hazard mitigation initiatives, an updated or new risk assessment, and changes in State or local priorities.

Visual 44

C1. Existing Policies and Programs

- The plan must document each jurisdiction's
  - Existing authorities
  - Policies, programs, and resources
  - Ability to expand on and improve existing policies and programs
- The plan might describe
  - Public works and/or emergency management staff
  - Zoning ordinances, building codes, subdivision regulation
  - Annual budgets
  - Comprehensive planning
  - Taxing authority

Visual 44

C1. Existing Policies and Programs

- The plan must document each jurisdiction's

  - o Existing authorities

  - o Policies, programs, and resources

  - o Ability to expand on and improve existing policies and programs

- The plan might describe

  - o Public works and/or emergency management staff

  - o Zoning ordinances, building codes, subdivision regulation

  - o Annual budgets

  - o Comprehensive planning

  - o Taxing authority

Plan reviewers look for a description of the capabilities and resources of each participating jurisdiction. Resources could include how much staff is available to work on mitigation, including planners, public works engineers, emergency management personnel, GIS staff, and floodplain managers. Capabilities can also be funding programs such as taxing authority and annual budgets.

Plan reviewers should look for plans and policies for each participating jurisdiction, such as comprehensive planning, building codes, zoning and subdivision ordinances, and stormwater management. Plan developers review existing plans, policies, and programs to identify plans that support or do not support the mitigation plan, policies that enable or present potential obstacles to mitigation, and programs that hinder or leverage the ability of the jurisdiction to implement mitigation actions.

The plan must include each jurisdiction's ability to expand on and improve its existing policies and programs.

This evaluation may result in mitigation actions to improve local capability.

Visual 45

C2. NFIP Participation

Does the plan address

- Participation in the NFIP?

- Continued compliance with NFIP requirements?

The plan could describe or discuss:

- Adoption and enforcement of floodplain management requirements

- Regulation of new construction in Special Flood Hazard Areas

- Need for updated maps for better identification of floodplains

- Floodplain management monitoring activities

 Photo shows an elevated house in the background that survived flooding in North Carolina and a non-elevated house in foreground that was damaged by flooding.

Visual 46

C3. Goals

- Does the plan include goals to reduce or avoid long-term vulnerabilities to identified hazards?
- Goals
  - Are broad policy statements
  - Must be consistent with the identified hazards

FEMA   Visual 46

C3. Goals

- Does the plan include goals to reduce or avoid long-term vulnerabilities to identified hazards?

- Goals

  - Are broad policy statements

  - Must be consistent with the identified hazards

Plan reviewers look for hazard mitigation goals for reducing or avoiding vulnerabilities to identified natural hazards.

Generally, goals are broad policy statements that explain what is to be achieved to reduce the risk of loss caused by natural hazards.

Plan reviewers look for consistency among the goals and the other parts of the plan, including the hazard identification and risk assessment.

However, plan reviewers will keep in mind Guiding Principle #4: Understand that this is the community's plan.

Photo shows a flooded road in West Virginia. A goal might be to avoid road closures in the future.

Visual 47

C4. Mitigation Actions

- The plan must identify and analyze a range of mitigation actions

- An action

  - Is an activity, process, or physical project designed to reduce or eliminate long-term risk to one or more hazards identified in the risk assessment?

- Does the plan include

  - Actions for new buildings and infrastructure?

  - Actions for existing buildings and infrastructure?

  - Actions for each jurisdiction?

For the plan to be approvable, plan reviewers must find actions that reduce risk to existing buildings and infrastructure.

For the plan to be approvable, plan reviewers must find actions that limit risk to new development and redevelopment.

The mitigation strategy must reflect the unique vulnerabilities and capabilities of the jurisdictions represented in the plan and reduce or avoid future losses.

Plan reviewers may find non-mitigation actions such as emergency preparedness or response actions in the plan; these are not mitigation actions, but plan reviewers do not require these types of actions to be removed from the plan.

Visual 48

C5. Action Plan

- The plan must contain an action plan
- For each jurisdiction, the plan must
  - Describe the criteria used for prioritizing implementation of mitigation actions
  - Demonstrate that the jurisdictions considered the benefits versus the costs
  - Identify who is responsible for implementing the action
  - Identify potential funding sources and expected timeframes for completion

Plan reviewers review the mitigation action plan and look for an explanation of how mitigation actions will be prioritized, implemented, and administered by each jurisdiction.

The plan must describe the criteria used for prioritizing actions and identify the responsible position, office, department, or agency responsible for implementing the actions for each jurisdiction as well as the potential funding sources and expected timeframes for completion.

As part of the prioritization process, the plan must demonstrate that the communities considered the costs versus the benefits of each action. A complete benefit-cost analysis is not required. Qualitative benefits, for example, quality of life, natural and beneficial values, or other benefits can also be included.

The intent is that as opportunities arise for actions to be implemented, each jurisdiction will be able to take action towards completion of their activities.

Visual 49

C6. Integration with Other Plans

- The plan must describe a process for integration

- Does the plan explain how mitigation will be integrated into
  - Other plans?
  - Ordinances?
  - Day-to-day operations?

- Is this provided for each jurisdiction?

Plan reviewers look for a description of how mitigation data, information, goals, and actions will be integrated with other planning mechanisms.

Planning mechanisms are governance structures that are used to manage local land use and development, such as budgets and day-to-day operations; capital improvement plans, comprehensive plans, stormwater management plans; the zoning ordinance or subdivision regulations; natural resource protection regulations, wildfire prevention, or open space management programs; or the flood damage prevention ordinance.

Plan reviewers look for a description of each participating jurisdiction's process for integration into their applicable planning mechanisms.

If the plan is an update, plan reviewers look for information about how integration into other planning mechanisms happened in the past as well as how incorporation will happen in the future.

Future plan integration may be included as a mitigation action.

 Photo shows a forest in Texas following a wildfire.

Visual 50

Element D. Plan Review, Evaluation, and Implementation

- This element is reviewed for plan UPDATES only
- The plan must reflect
  - Changes in development
  - Progress in mitigation
  - Changes in priorities
- The plan must be resubmitted for approval every 5 years
- Intent of Element D
  - The plan continues to be relevant
  - The plan reflects current conditions

Plan reviewers complete this section of the Plan Review Tool for plan updates only. Updates are required every 5 years to maintain eligibility for FEMA mitigation grant funding.

The plan update is an opportunity for each jurisdiction to describe changes in development, progress in implementing mitigation efforts, and changes in community priorities.

The purpose of updating a plan is to ensure that the mitigation strategy remains relevant to the community needs, capabilities, and vulnerabilities. A mitigation plan must represent current conditions and current vulnerabilities as well as take into consideration possible future conditions that can impact the vulnerability of the community.

Plan reviewers understand that if little has changed in a community since the earlier mitigation plan was developed, much of the data and text in the updated plan will be unchanged. This is acceptable. Plan reviewers look for documentation of progress or changes in the hazard mitigation programs and for continued engagement in the mitigation planning process.

Visual 51

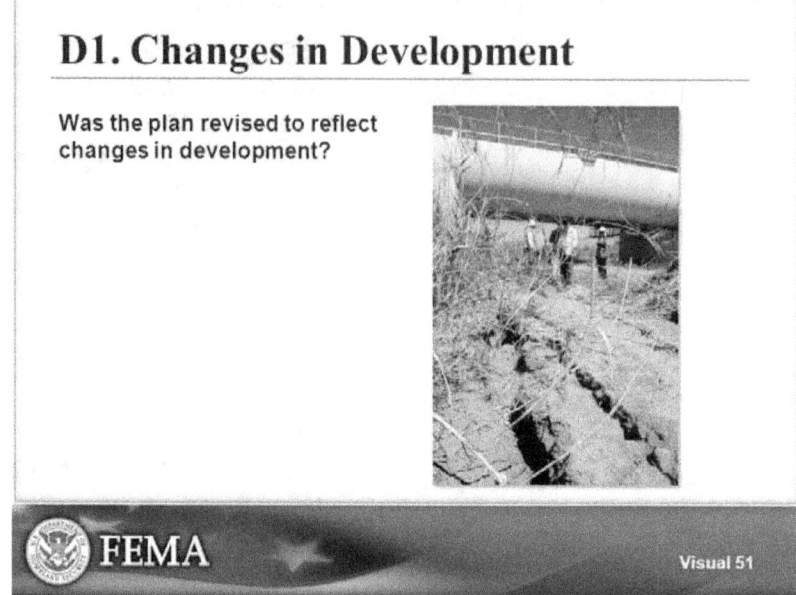

D1. Changes in Development

Was the plan revised to reflect changes in development?

Plan reviewers look for a description of changes in development in hazard-prone areas. Changes in development means new construction, planned development, or changes in conditions that affect risk, such as climate variability, declining population, increasing population, foreclosures, and so forth. The plan must explain whether new development has increased or decreased the vulnerability of each jurisdiction since the last plan was approved. As appropriate, the plan may show trends in vulnerability or in development in hazard-prone locations.

Not all changes in development will affect vulnerability. If changes in development have not affected vulnerability, plan reviewers look for validation of the information contained in the previously approved plan.

Photo shows an irrigation canal in California that was damaged by an earthquake.

Visual 52

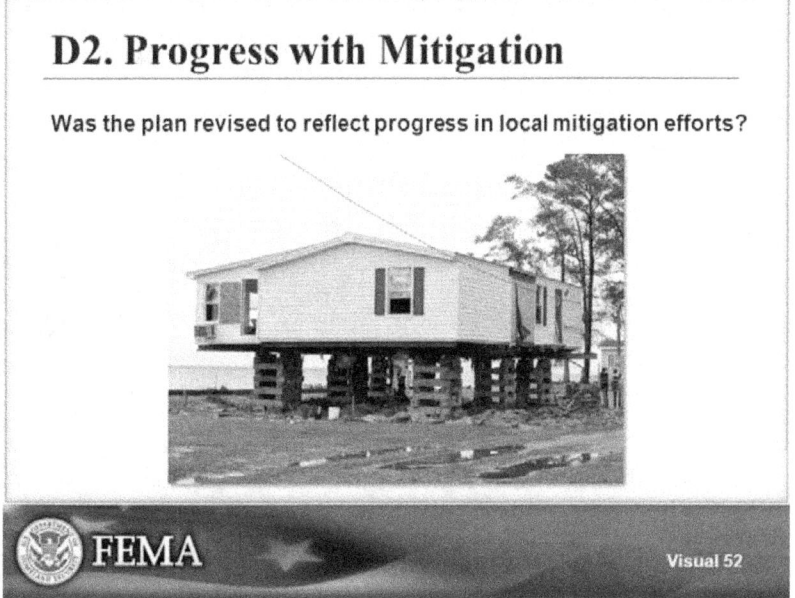

D2. Progress with Mitigation

Was the plan revised to reflect progress in local mitigation efforts?

Achieving goals and implementing the mitigation strategy can change overall vulnerability in a jurisdiction.

Plan reviewers look for information about the status of the mitigation actions proposed in the previous plan. The plan must identify actions that have been completed as well as those that are not completed. For actions that have not been completed, plan reviewers look for an explanation as to whether the action is no longer relevant and will be deleted from the action plan or continues to be relevant and is included in the updated action plan.

 Photo shows an elevation project in North Carolina.

Visual 53

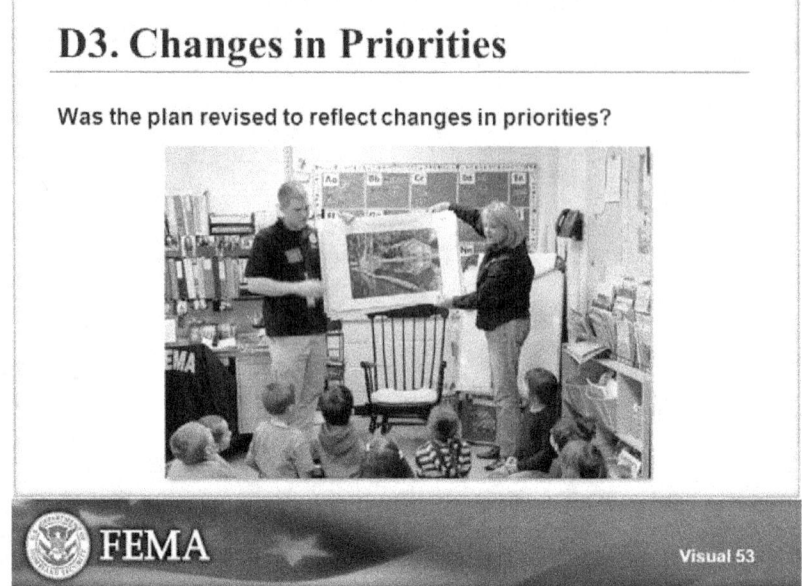

D3. Changes in Priorities

Was the plan revised to reflect changes in priorities?

The plan must describe if and how any mitigation priorities changed since the plan was previously approved. Plan reviewers look for an explanation of changed priorities or, if no changes in priorities were found to be necessary, validation of the information in the previously approved plan. Plan reviewers look not only for changes in vulnerabilities that have led to a change in priorities, but also to changes in regulations, policies, and financial opportunities, as well as post-disaster conditions that may affect mitigation priorities.

 Photo shows a public education activity in New York State.

Visual 54

Element E. Plan Adoption

- The plan must include documentation of adoption

- For multi-jurisdictional plans, each jurisdiction must adopt

- Intent of Element E

    o Adoption demonstrates commitment

    o Adoption legitimizes the plan

- Updated plans must be adopted anew

For final approval of the plan, FEMA must receive documentation of formal adoption by appropriate governing bodies.

For a multi-jurisdictional plan, the plan is only effective in a particular jurisdiction if the appropriate governing body of that jurisdiction has adopted the plan.

The purpose of adoption is to ensure that elected officials are aware of the plan, support the mitigation goals, and authorize implementation of the plan.

Note that updated plans must be adopted just as the first mitigation plan developed by a community must be adopted.

Visual 55

E1. Documentation of Adoption

- The plan must include documentation of adoption
- Does the plan include a
  - Signed resolution?
  - Other evidence?

Plan approvers look for documentation of adoption such as a signed resolution. In lieu of a signed resolution, a community may provide evidence of formal adoption in another way depending on local law. The Plan Review Guide includes some information about alternative documentation of adoption.

To demonstrate the commitment of individual jurisdictions to fulfilling their mitigation goals and to authorize responsible agencies to implement mitigation actions, each jurisdiction must formally adopt the plan. Note that formal adoption must take place within 1 calendar year of the plan having received "Approvable Pending Adoption" status.

 Photo shows officials signing documents in California.

Visual 56

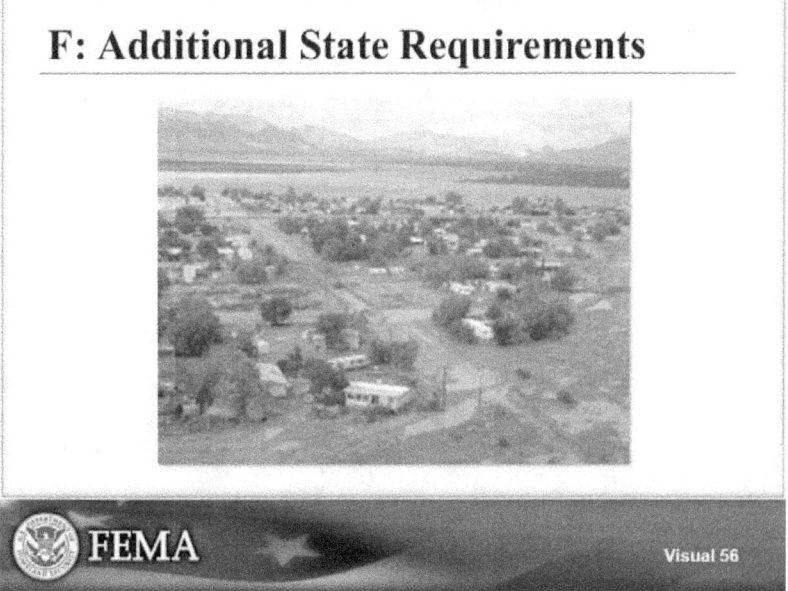

F: Additional State Requirements

States may have additional planning requirements. For example, a State might require that certain local officials be invited to participate in the planning process and the plan must document that these invitations were issued. Or a State might require that information about potential mitigation projects be submitted in a particular format in the plan to facilitate tracking by the State.

 Photo shows a town in Arizona after a flood.

Visual 57

> ## Required Revisions
>
> - Sub-elements consolidated
> - Plan approvers explain
>   - Which sub-elements do not meet requirements
>   - Why the information is required
>   - What can be done to meet the requirements
> - Example
>   - The plan does not explain how neighboring jurisdictions and other interested parties were given an opportunity to participate in the development of this plan. Describe the opportunities provided to these groups and explain how they were involved in the process.
>
>  FEMA
>
> Visual 57

Required Revisions

- Sub-elements consolidated

- Plan approvers explain

  - Which sub-elements do not meet requirements

  - Why the information is required

  - What can be done to meet the requirements

- Example

  - The plan does not explain how neighboring jurisdictions and other interested parties were given an opportunity to participate in the development of this plan. Describe the opportunities provided to these groups and explain how they were involved in the process.

For each element, the plan approver must explain why particular sub-elements of the plan do not meet requirements. There is space on the Plan Review Tool below each sub-element for explanation of required revisions for the entire element. Plan approvers must explain why the information is required and should review the Plan Review Guide and information about the intent of the element to develop this explanation.

Plan approvers explain how to meet the requirement using concise and precise statements.

Here is a brief example of an entry in the "Required Revisions" box on the Regulation Checklist; note that the example both states the shortcoming of the plan and explains how to overcome this shortcoming.

Visual 58

Questions?

- This section covered these elements
  - Planning Process
  - Hazard Identification and Risk Assessment
  - Mitigation Strategy
  - Plan Review, Evaluation, and Implementation
  - Plan Adoption
  - Additional State Requirements
- Questions?

Visual 58

Questions?

- This section covered these elements
  - Planning Process
  - Hazard Identification and Risk Assessment
  - Mitigation Strategy
  - Plan Review, Evaluation, and Implementation
  - Plan Adoption
  - Additional State Requirements
- Questions?

This section considered each of the sections of the Regulation Checklist. This section has addressed the third course objective and participants should now understand how to use the Plan Review Tool. This section also addressed the fourth objective of the course and participants should now understand how to convey an effective plan evaluation using the Regulation Checklist. The next section of the course discusses using the Plan Assessment portion of the Plan Review Tool.

Are there any questions?

Photo shows coastal erosion in California.

Section 5. Plan Assessment

Time: 30 minutes

OBJECTIVES

At the end of this unit, participants will be able to:

- Describe how to convey the results of the review using the Plan Assessment

METHODOLOGY

This unit includes lecture and provides opportunity to participants for asking questions.

Visual 59

5. Plan Assessment

- Intent of Plan Assessment

  - To offer more comprehensive feedback on plan quality

- The Plan Assessment has two parts

  - A. Plan Strengths and Opportunities for Improvement

  - B. Resources for Implementation

The Plan Assessment is the plan approver's opportunity to communicate to the local community. The audience may include plan developers, local planners, elected officials, and other stakeholders. This audience may appreciate receiving not only information about how the plan does or does not comply with Federal regulations through the Regulation Checklist, but also information about ways in which the plan is strong, opportunities for improving the plan, and resources for implementing the plan.

The Plan Assessment is also an opportunity for the State to inform the community of State funding priorities and technical assistance opportunities.

The Plan Assessment has two parts:

- Part A includes questions that encourage the plan approver to comment on strengths and weaknesses of the plan.

- Part B includes questions that encourage the plan approver to provide information about resources for implementing the mitigation strategy.

Visual 60

Element A. Planning Process

- How does the plan go above and beyond minimum requirements?

- Does the plan demonstrate

    o Broad involvement of stakeholders?

    o Involvement of a large number of local agencies?

    o Diverse methods of public participation?

    o Open and inclusive public involvement process?

- How can the planning process be improved in future plan updates?

Plan approvers can comment on how the planning process was effective and resulted in vigorous community involvement. Approvers consider the use of diverse methods of public participation, and ways in which the planning process was open and inclusive. Alternatively, the plan approver may want to suggest innovative ways to improve public participation in future plan updates.

Visual 61

Element B. Hazard Identification and Risk Assessment

- Does the risk assessment include information about

  o Future development trends?

  o Existing structures and infrastructure?

  o Future structures and infrastructure?

  o Estimated dollar losses for each hazard?

  o Methods used to develop the estimates?

- Does the plan demonstrate

  o Use of best available data?

  o Communication of risk to the public?

Plan approvers should consider each of the questions listed on Page A-6, and as appropriate, respond. Some of the questions are:

- Does the risk assessment describe land use and future development trends?

- Does the plan provide detail about the types and number of existing structures and infrastructure in hazard-prone areas?

- Does the plan consider future as well as existing structures and infrastructure?

- Does the plan provide an estimate of potential losses for each hazard and explain how the estimates were developed?

- Does the plan use best available data and demonstrate communication of risk to the public?

When providing comments about the risk assessment, plan approvers should be as helpful as possible, for instance, by suggesting specific locations for where to find better data and how the data could be used to improve the vulnerability analysis. The data has to be useful for the community, so plan approvers might explain how specific methodologies could be used to improve their understanding of their risks and develop mitigation actions.

Visual 62

Element C. Mitigation Strategy

- How well does the plan
  - Reflect the vulnerability assessment?
  - Set goals based on problems?
  - Provide a diversity of actions?
- Plan approver may suggest opportunities for implementation

Element C. Mitigation Strategy

- How well does the plan

  o Reflect the vulnerability assessment?

  o Set goals based on problems?

  o Provide a diversity of actions?

- Plan approver may suggest opportunities for implementation

Plan approvers should comment on strengths of the plan with respect to how well the mitigation strategies address the vulnerabilities identified in the risk assessment. Other considerations include how well the plan's goals are based on the unique circumstances of the communities and how the mitigation strategy includes actions to address future development. Plan approvers may want to suggest opportunities for implementing the proposed mitigation actions to improve the integration of the plan into other mechanisms or address other areas of the plan that could be improved with the next plan update, such as improved floodplain analyses.

Photo shows a drainage project in Virginia.

Visual 63

Element D. Plan Update, Evaluation, and Implementation

- How does the plan document the 5-year evaluation with respect to
  - Status of mitigation actions?
  - Identification of obstacles to implementation of actions?
  - Solutions for overcoming the obstacles?
  - Reduction of risk?

FEMA   Visual 63

Element D. Plan Update, Evaluation, and Implementation

- How does the plan document the 5-year evaluation with respect to

  o Status of mitigation actions?

  o Identification of obstacles to implementation of actions?

  o Solutions for overcoming the obstacles?

  o Reduction of risk?

For each part of the Plan Assessment, the Plan Review Guide provides a list of possible considerations.

Part D of the Plan Assessment provides the opportunity for plan approvers to comment on the strengths of an updated plan relative to plan update, plan evaluation, and implementation of mitigation actions. For plan updates only, plan approvers consider questions such as how does the plan explain the status of mitigation actions, obstacles to implementing mitigation actions, solutions for overcoming obstacles, or risks that have been avoided or reduced as a result of mitigation?

Visual 64

Plan Assessment Discussion

- Plan Assessment should

    o Provide a synopsis of overall strengths of the plan

    o Provide suggestions, not directions

    o Be relevant to the plan

        – Sections may be left blank

- Delete *italicized* questions before completing

- Remember Guiding Principle #5

    o The plan review should foster relationships

The Plan Assessment should be a short synopsis of the overall strengths and weaknesses of the Plan and opportunities for improving the plan in the future. It should not be a complete recap of each section of the plan and it should not repeat any of the information in the Regulation Checklist.

Plan approvers enter comments in the Plan Assessment that suggest modifications rather than direct the community to make the changes.

If there are no pertinent comments, the sections pertaining to strengths and opportunities may be left blank.

The plan reviewer should delete the *italicized* questions printed in the Plan Assessment; the questions are included to guide the plan reviewer.

If plan reviewer comments are very complicated, the plan reviewer should consider whether a phone call would be more productive.

The plan reviewer should remember Guiding Principle #5 that the plan review should foster relationships by providing constructive and positive feedback.

Visual 65

Resources for Implementation

- FEMA funding programs
- Other Federal programs
- Publications, technical guidance
- Upcoming trainings or workshops

Visual 65

Resources for Implementation

- FEMA funding programs
- Other Federal programs
- Publications, technical guidance
- Upcoming trainings or workshops

Plan reviewers *together with the State Hazard Mitigation Officer* may want to suggest opportunities for implementing the proposed mitigation actions. This doesn't replace the implementation requirements that must be included in the plan.

Suggestions that may be helpful to local jurisdictions include information about FEMA funding, other Federal programs, publications, guidance, upcoming workshops, and so forth. Information can be provided about the Community Rating System (CRS) and the NFIP, as well as about programs administered by other Federal agencies such as the U. S. Forest Service, National Oceanic and Atmospheric Administration, Environmental Protection Agency (on Smart Growth), and the U.S. Department of Housing and Urban Development (on Sustainable Communities).

Plan reviewers may provide links to or information about published documents or studies pertinent to hazards and/or mitigation and may provide information about upcoming training or workshops such as a Benefit-Cost Analysis (BCA) training workshop. The State plan reviewer may be the best person to complete this section, specifically related to State-sponsored trainings and State-administered grant programs.

The resources included in this section should be unique to the mitigation strategy found in the plan and reflect the capabilities of the participating jurisdictions. The intent is to move the communities towards implementation of their plan.

 Photo shows snow being plowed after a blizzard in Colorado.

Visual 66

Good Example of Plan Assessment Comment

The plan links the results of the risk assessment directly to goals and to proposed mitigation actions. The community can use the results of the risk assessment to develop applications for mitigation project funding.

The comment

- Identifies a strength of the plan
- Suggests an opportunity for using the information developed during the planning process to apply for mitigation funding
- Is consistent with the Guiding Principle to Focus on the Mitigation Strategy

Visual 67

Not a Good Example of Plan Assessment Comment

> There is no clear connection between the risk assessment and the mitigation actions listed in this plan. Plan developers should find a workshop on developing a mitigation plan and attend it before resubmitting the plan for review.

- The comment
  - Does not provide information about an opportunity for improvement
  - May actually belong as a required revision in the Regulation Checklist
  - Is not helpful in building a relationship with the local community and, therefore, violates one of the Guiding Principles

FEMA   Visual 67

Not a Good Example of Plan Assessment Comment

There is no clear connection between the risk assessment and the mitigation actions listed in this plan. Plan developers should find a workshop on developing a mitigation plan and attend it before resubmitting the plan for review.

The comment

- Does not provide information about an opportunity for improvement
- May actually belong as a required revision in the Regulation Checklist
- Is not helpful in building a relationship with the local community and, therefore, violates one of the Guiding Principles

Visual 68

Questions?

- This section provided information about

  - How to relay feedback about strengths and opportunities for improvement

  - Ideas for resources for implementing the plan

- Questions?

This section provided information about using the Plan Assessment to discuss strengths of the plan and provide information about resources or opportunities. This section addressed the fourth objective of the course and participants should now understand how to convey an effective plan evaluation using the Plan Assessment.

Are there any questions?

 Photo shows a public meeting in American Samoa.

Section 6. Wrap-Up and Post-Course Assessment

Time: 30 minutes

OBJECTIVES

At the end of this unit, participants will be able to:

- Review course goals and objectives
- Ask questions and clarify remaining issues
- Assess understanding of the concepts presented in this course

METHODOLOGY

This unit includes lecture and provides opportunity to participants for asking questions.

Visual 69

Additional Resources

- For further information about mitigation planning:
  https://www.fema.gov/multi-hazard-mitigation-planning

- For information about mitigation plan procedures:
  https://www.fema.gov/risk-mapping-assessment-planning/regional-contact-information

- For information about implementing a mitigation plan:
  https://www.fema.gov/media-library/assets/documents/34953

Thank you for taking the Plan Review for Local Mitigation Plans course. To assist you during a plan review, consult the *Local Mitigation Plan Review Guide*. Consult these Web sites for current mitigation planning information.

Visual 70

6. Wrap-Up and Post-Course Assessment

This course briefly reviewed the

1. Background of hazard mitigation planning

2. Guiding Principles

3. The Plan Review Tool

4. Regulation Checklist

5. Plan Assessment

Questions?

 FEMA   Visual 70

6. Wrap-Up and Post-Course Assessment

This course briefly reviewed the

1.   Background of hazard mitigation planning

2.   Guiding Principles

3.   The Plan Review Tool

4.   Regulation Checklist

5.   Plan Assessment

Questions?

The course briefly reviewed information that plan reviewers need to know and to keep in mind when reviewing a plan. Plan reviewers must refer to the Plan Review Guide throughout the plan review for further information about the intent of Federal regulations, examples of how plans can meet the intent of the regulations, and issues to consider during a review. We have discussed the background of mitigation planning, Guiding Principles, the Plan Review Tool, the Regulation Checklist, and the Plan Assessment.

Are there any questions?

Post-Course Assessment Answer Key
Plan Review for Local Mitigation Plans
Correct answer shown in **Bold**
Select 10 questions for a Post-Course Assessment; select some questions for each course objective

Objective A Questions

1. Which of the following best describes the purpose of reviewing a local hazard mitigation plan?
   a. **To determine whether the plan meets the requirements of 44 CFR 201.6**
   b. To determine whether the plan is consistent with current practice and philosophy of planning
   c. To determine whether the plan meets the requirements of 44 CFR 59.1
   d. To learn how the local community has saved money by mitigating the potential effects of natural and human-caused hazards

2. Which of the following is NOT a reason to review a local hazard mitigation plan?
   a. **To disqualify a community from receiving Hazard Mitigation Assistance grant funds**
   b. To provide current information to the community about mitigation funding opportunities
   c. To provide current information to the community about hazard mitigation or flood insurance training and technical assistance opportunities
   d. To qualify a community for applying for and receiving Hazard Mitigation Assistance grant funds

3. Which of the following actions would be consistent with the Guiding Principles?
   a. **Accept the planning process as defined by the local community**
   b. Postpone the plan review because the community's eligibility for receiving Hazard Mitigation Assistance grant funds does not expire for another 12 months
   c. Do not respond to questions about the plan review posed by the State because plan review is a FEMA responsibility
   d. Require modifications in the organization of the plan so that information is presented in the order that questions are asked in the Regulatory Checklist; this will facilitate the final review

4. Which of the following actions would NOT be consistent with the Guiding Principles?
   a. **Focus the review on the methodology used for estimating the potential cost of future damage and look for ways to deny approval of the plan**
   b. Accept the planning process as defined by the local community
   c. Review the plan to validate compliance with the intent of mitigation planning regulations
   d. Work with the State to ensure that the plan review is communicated clearly and is completed in a timely manner

5. FEMA uses a *performance-based* approach rather than a *prescriptive* approach when publishing mitigation planning guidance, meaning that FEMA generally focuses *what* should be done in the process and documented in the plan, rather than specifying exactly *how* it should be done.
   a. **TRUE**
   b. FALSE

6. Mitigation planning requirements together with various FEMA guidance documents specify not only *what* should be part of the process but, more importantly, exactly *how* the process should be carried out.
   a. TRUE
   b. **FALSE**

7. A sound hazard identification and risk assessment is actually more important than the proposed mitigation action strategy.
   a. TRUE
   b. **FALSE**

8. A plan that describes a complicated planning process makes for a stronger and better plan than a plan that describes a relatively simple planning process.
   a. TRUE
   b. **FALSE**

9. Plan reviewers use the *Local Mitigation Plan Review Guide* to ensure that local mitigation plans meet the requirements of the Stafford Act and Title 44 Code of Federal Regulations Section 201.6.
   a. **TRUE**
   b. FALSE

10. FEMA reviews local plans to foster federal, state, and local partnerships for hazard mitigation; promote more resilient and sustainable communities; and reduce the costs associated with disaster response and recovery by promoting hazard mitigation activities.
   a. **TRUE**
   b. FALSE

Objective B Questions

9. Which of the following activities would a reviewer expect to read about as part of the mitigation planning process?
   a. **Posting information about planning meetings on the community Web site and conducting mitigation planning workshops**
   b. Developing detailed blueprints for construction of a large community safe room
   c. Obtaining cost proposals from a number of qualified bidders for installation of hurricane shutters on all public buildings in the planning area
   d. Surveying local residents about levels of education, income, and marital status

10. Which of the following would a reviewer identify as mitigation actions?
   a. Purchasing new fire trucks and other emergency response vehicles

b. **Elevating structures in a floodplain and clearing flammable materials away from structures in a wildfire-prone area**

c. Conducting an exercise to test the Emergency Action Plan developed for a dam in the planning area

d. Clearing debris from roadways following an ice storm

11. Which of the following would be most appropriate for documenting that the public was provided an opportunity to participate during the drafting stage of the planning process?

a. Minutes of a public meeting where hazard mitigation planning was not discussed

b. Sign-in sheets from an open house held at the local library to celebrate the opening of a new children's library

c. **Sign-in sheets from open meetings about mitigation planning and copies of comments received about the draft plan through an interactive Web site**

d. Photograph of a public meeting from the FEMA Photo Library

12. Plan reviewers can approve a plan that omits consideration of a natural hazard from the planning process even if the hazard is commonly recognized as having the potential to occur in the planning area.

a. TRUE

b. **FALSE**

13. Plan reviewers look for information about other community planning mechanisms in the plan because mitigation goals, objectives, and actions could conceivably become an integral part of the Local Comprehensive Plan, Community Economic Development Plan, and the Community Post-Disaster Recovery Plan.

a. **TRUE**

b. FALSE

14. Which of the following best describes the information that a plan reviewer would expect to find in an updated mitigation plan?

a. Copy of zoning regulations adopted since the last plan was approved

b. Copy of a newspaper article about an Emergency Management Department building constructed in the community since the last plan was approved

c. Names, titles, and affiliations of government officials elected since the last plan was approved

d. **Summary of mitigation actions that have been completed and information about new development that has occurred in hazard-prone locations since the last plan was approved**

15. Plan reviewers look for documentation of how stakeholders and the public were invited to participate in the planning process.

a. **TRUE**

b. FALSE

16. When reviewing the risk assessment, plan reviewers look for proof that the community used the most sophisticated technologies currently approved by FEMA; otherwise, plan reviewers do not considered the conclusions of the risk assessment to be accurate.
    a. TRUE
    b. **FALSE**

17. When reviewing the mitigation strategy, plan reviewers look for proof that the community used the FEMA Benefit-Cost Analysis software to determine if each proposed action will be cost effective.
    a. TRUE
    b. **FALSE**

18. The plan must address natural hazards. Human-caused or technological hazards may be addressed in the local mitigation plan, but these are not required.
    a. **TRUE**
    b. FALSE

19. FEMA plan reviewers should require that extraneous information be removed from a plan, including information about technological hazards, prior to plan approval.
    a. TRUE
    b. **FALSE**

20. When reviewing an updated plan, the plan reviewer looks for information about hazards events that have occurred since the last plan was developed.
    a. **TRUE**
    b. FALSE

21. When reviewing a multi-jurisdictional plan, a plan reviewer will not accept a statement that a hazard such as extreme heat can affect the "entire planning area" as an adequate description of the location of a hazard.
    a. TRUE
    b. **FALSE**

22. Plan reviewers believe that the local hazard mitigation plan is a unique and standalone planning mechanism. Although plans typically include information about other local plans, plan reviewers do not look for information about how information from these other plans or studies was incorporated into the mitigation plan.
    a. TRUE
    b. **FALSE**

23. The Regulation Checklist leads the plan reviewer through systematic consideration of each required element of a local hazard mitigation plan.
    a. **TRUE**
    b. FALSE

24. The purpose of the plan review is to offer more comprehensive feedback on the quality of the plan, provide suggestions for improvement, identify strengths of the plan, and include recommendations for implementing the plan.
    a. **TRUE**
    b. FALSE

25. When reviewing the planning process, the plan reviewer looks for evidence of involvement of top elected public officials and will approve a plan even if there is no documentation of public involvement opportunities.
    a. TRUE
    b. **FALSE**

26. When reviewing an updated mitigation plan, the plan reviewer knows that the public was involved in developing the earlier, approved version of the plan and understands that there is no requirement for public involvement in the process of updating the plan.
    a. TRUE
    b. **FALSE**

27. Plan reviewers look for a schedule and method for keeping the plan current by monitoring or tracking the implementation of mitigation actions and evaluating the effectiveness of the plan in achieving its stated goals.
    a. **TRUE**
    b. FALSE

28. For a multi-jurisdictional plan, only the hazards that have the potential to affect the entire planning area must be identified and analyzed in the plan.
    a. TRUE
    b. **FALSE**

29. Plan reviewers believe that the purpose of listing existing community plans, policies, and programs is to demonstrate that a community possesses the technical capability to develop a high-quality local hazard mitigation plan.
    a. TRUE
    b. **FALSE**

30. For a multi-jurisdictional plan, a single mitigation strategy is always sufficient because all of the jurisdictions will generally face the same hazards and have similar capabilities for implementing mitigation actions.
    a. TRUE
    b. **FALSE**

Objective C Questions

31. Which of the following statements are appropriate for the Plan Assessment?
    a. **The plan uses Hazus to produce estimates of losses due to flooding even though this level of study is not required by planning regulations.**
    b. The area clearly needs a new hydrologic and hydraulic study because the areas that are flooded seem to be increasing in acreage every year.
    c. The plan fails to describe the location of floodprone areas.
    d. The plan should include photographs to show the level of damage from the most recent floods.

32. Which of the following would be an appropriate comment regarding a REQUIRED REVISION?
    a. The plan is poorly worded and difficult to follow and must be rewritten.
    b. The plan does not meet sub-element B1 and must be revised so that it complies with Federal planning regulations.
    c. This section of the plan is imprecise.
    d. **The plan does not meet sub-element B1 because it does not identify locations within the planning area that may experience a landslide. If the entire planning area is prone to landslides, state this. If only some parts of the planning area are prone to landslides, describe these locations in a narrative (e.g., landslide areas are the hillsides along the north side of State Route 6 between Alpha Road and Beta Street) or include a map that identifies these locations.**

33. If a planning element is not met, the reviewer must explain the shortcomings in the box titled "REQUIRED REVISIONS" and provide a clear explanation of the revisions that are necessary for plan approval.
    a. **TRUE**
    b. FALSE

34. The following paragraph is appropriate for a plan reviewer to enter in the Plan Assessment section of the Plan Review Tool:
    "The plan contains excellent information on funding sources and resources for implementing mitigation actions. It may also be useful to include contact information for the State Hazard Mitigation Office among these resources since the State is responsible for coordinating the implementation of many of these programs within the State."
    a. **TRUE**
    b. FALSE

35. The following paragraphs are appropriate for a plan reviewer to enter in the Plan Assessment section of the Plan Review Tool:
    "Plan Strength: The updated plan lists dates of annual plan monitoring and evaluation meetings over the past 5 years. Section 7.4 states that the plan will continue to be reviewed annually to monitor progress of the mitigation actions.

    "Opportunity for Improvement: The Plan lists mitigation actions that were proposed in the previous plan but were not implemented. It would be useful if the plan described obstacles that prevented progress on mitigation actions so that these may be addressed more fully when the plan is next updated."

    a. **TRUE**
    b. FALSE

36. The following paragraph is appropriate for a plan reviewer to enter in the Plan Assessment section of the Plan Review Tool:

> "The plan lists critical structures in the community, but does nothing with this information such as estimating losses that would be incurred should each of the identified hazards occur. This is a weakness that shows a lack of understanding of the purpose of a mitigation plan. "

    a. TRUE
    b. **FALSE**

37. The following sentence is appropriate for a plan reviewer to enter in the Plan Assessment section of the Plan Review Tool:

> "Potential dollar loss estimates are not addressed in this plan but would be a good addition to the next update."

    a. **TRUE**
    b. FALSE

38. The following comment is appropriate for a plan reviewer to enter in the Plan Assessment section of the Plan Review Tool:

> "The plan says that there has been no new development in the planning area in the past decade, which is completely unreasonable. Think about new roads as well as new residential and commercial development in the area and revise this section of the plan so that it can be approved."

    a. TRUE
    b. **FALSE**

39. The purpose of the Plan Assessment is to offer the local community more comprehensive narrative feedback on the quality and utility of the plan for future consideration.

    a. **TRUE**
    b. FALSE

40. The purpose of the Plan Assessment is to criticize elements of the plan that are not required by law.

    a. TRUE
    b. **FALSE**